LAZY LAMA LOOKS AT
The Six Paramitas

RINGU TULKU RINPOCHE

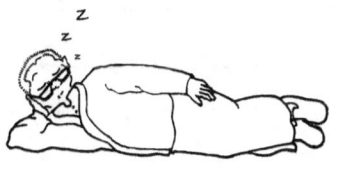

Number 8 in the Lazy Lama series

First Published in 2021 by Bodhicharya Publications
Bodhicharya Publications is a Community Interest Company registered in the UK.
38 Moreland Avenue, Hereford, HR1 1BN, UK
www.bodhicharya.org   email: publications@bodhicharya.org

Text ©Bodhicharya Publications

Ringu Tulku asserts the moral right to be identified as the author of this work. Please do not reproduce any part of this book without permission from the publisher.

ISBN 978-0-9957343-4-0

First Edition. 2021.

Transcribed and edited by Karma Trinley Paldron.
From teachings given at at Gaunts House, Dorset UK, and Karma Dzong, Paris.
Illustrations by Karma Orgyen Namdreul.

Typesetting & Design by Paul O'Connor at Judo Design, Ireland.

Cover Image: Conrad Harvey
Lazy Lama logo: Conrad Harvey & Rebecca O'Connor

Contents

Editor's Preface	vii
Introduction	1
1. Generosity	13
2. Shila / Discipline	41
3. Patience	83
4. Diligence	125
5. Meditation	165
6. Wisdom	207
Acknowledgements	249
About the Author	251

Editor's Preface

The Six Paramitas, or "transcendent perfections," contain all the skills needed for taming the mind and opening the heart.

Paramita is a Sanskrit word. *Para* means "beyond" and "the further shore" and *mita*, means "that which has arrived." So, broadly speaking, *Pāramitā*, means "that which has gone to the further shore."

For beginners, "the further shore" seems very far away. We can feel overwhelmed before we even set out. But in this, the eighth book of the Lazy Lama series, Ringu Tulku Rinpoche helps us to understand how the path of the bodhisattva is possible for all of us.

In providing this wonderful bridge on the journey from here to the further shore, Rinpoche reveals the Six Paramitas as bodhicitta in action, rather than an unattainable state of perfection. Through his wisdom and great compassion, warm humour and unfailing patience, Rinpoche shows us how these profound teachings are essential to our lives, especially in these times of stress and great uncertainty.

Karma Trinley Paldron
Dublin, 2021

Introduction

It seems that so many things in this world are not going in the right direction, so I would like to say something about what we can do to make our world a better place to live. I think everything that we need to improve our world, our society and our humanity is in the Six Paramitas. These practices can be very useful for making our life temporarily good, as well as bringing lasting peace and happiness.

"*Paramita*" is a Sanskrit word, meaning that from this samsaric state of being, we cross over to nirvana. "*Para*" means the other side and "*mita*" means going to the other side. So that is Paramita, going from samsara to enlightenment.

The Six Paramitas is the practical training of the Bodhisattva's path. In English, it is sometimes translated as "perfection." I think what it means is to perfect these six positive trainings.

As this is the practice of *Mahayana*, or *Bodhisattvayana*, maybe we need to say a few words about the *Bodhisattva*, which is also a Sanskrit word. *Bodhi* is sometimes translated as enlightenment, from the root word *bodh*, "to know." It means knowing completely how things are. *Bodhi* is the knowledge of wisdom, of awakening, free from confusion and ignorance, and "*sattva*" is somebody who has heart, or courage. So, a person who has the heart or the courage for awakening is called a Bodhisattva; and this awakening is not only of yourself, but of everybody.

Therefore, somebody who has the strong aspiration to end the sufferings of all beings and bring lasting peace and happiness to everybody, however difficult it may be and however long it might take, is called a bodhisattva.

It is an approach based on compassion, on the attitude of wishing to help not only myself, but all of us together. The attitude is not "I and you," but "me and we." I see everybody as "we." Just as I myself want to be free from pain and suffering and problems, so do all sentient beings. And just as I want to be happy, joyful, and have all the positive things of life not just for a short time, but forever, so I also know that everybody wants the same thing.

We so wish all our near and dear ones to have happiness and be free from suffering that we often sacrifice a lot for them. This is not something foreign to us; it is done all the time. Everywhere in the world people are ready to sacrifice their lives to protect their family, their community, their country and their religion. In doing that, however, there is always a limitation.

When we have concepts, our limitations and our boundaries become very strong. We limit this love, this compassion, this willingness to help, to *our* side. The main reason is because we do not include everybody in this feeling of "we." We say "I," and "we," and we protect what is ours *against* others. Sometimes we make others so horrible and insignificant that we don't mind giving them all kinds of pain and suffering and torture. But if you look a little bit deeper, you will understand that they are not different from us.

I saw a film on the Rwanda massacre. People of one community were going with big, terrible swords, searching for the others, and saying, "Where are the cockroaches?" They were looking for people who were actually the same as themselves, but out of ignorance, out of a certain kind of hatred or wrong way of seeing, they were projecting what people think of as the worst kind of insect onto others, and then killing them. Because if you see people as nothing more than cockroaches then you have less of a problem, or maybe even no problem, to crush them.

From the bodhisattva's point of view, that is not the way. Everybody is the same and has the same feelings. Like us, they want to love and be loved and they also feel the same way for their own near and dear ones.

Although "bodhisattva" may be a Buddhist word, in fact there are bodhisattvas everywhere, including animals, birds, fishes and insects. Why not? Anybody who has that kind of aspiration, or attitude, is called a bodhisattva.

In the Jataka Stories, it is said that Buddha took countless lifetimes before he became Buddha. Even after he became a bodhisattva, he took lots of different life forms. Sometimes he was a bodhisattva deer, or an elephant. Sometimes he was a monkey, or different kinds of birds...and sometimes even rabbits.

Once, when the Bodhisattva was a very kind, compassionate rabbit, he saw a hungry person, sick and alone in the forest, in great anguish and crying for help.

The rabbit said, "What do you want?"

The man said, "I want food. I haven't eaten. I'm going to die if I don't get food."

So the rabbit said, "What do you eat?"

"I eat meat. I'm a hunter. I couldn't get any meat so therefore I am dying."

The rabbit said, "Okay, you just make a fire and maybe you will get some meat."

So the hunter made a fire, and when his fire was very, very strong and very, very big, the rabbit ran quickly and jumped into the fire and he gave his body to this man.

So that is the rabbit bodhisattva. That is the main understanding from the Buddhist point of view.

Even if we don't have that kind of natural compassion for every being, we can learn, we can understand and we can train. To see the importance of being a bodhisattva, to generate the bodhisattva's attitude and then to become one, is the strongest, most positive practice.

It is said that if you become a bodhisattva, you will become a Buddha sooner or later. There is no alternative. Just as a crown prince is sure to become the next king, in the same way a bodhisattva is sure to become a Buddha, even if he or she doesn't want to become one.

Many bodhisattvas like Chenrezig make a promise to themselves, "I will never, ever become a Buddha until I have led every being to Buddhahood without exception and without leaving anyone behind. Only then will I become Buddha."

«Once, the Buddha was a very kind, compassionate rabbit.»

When you have so much compassion and so much wisdom, you are a Buddha whether you like it or not. You want to transform yourself, but you think what is the use if you alone are free of problems. You have to make sure that everyone else is free also. Their cause is as dear to you as your own cause.

I have to transform myself first, otherwise I cannot help. I have to learn how to be free from suffering and pain and the problems of samsara. I have to learn how to deal with my own emotions and negative habitual tendencies and see things in a clear way. So therefore, first I need to train in order to help others. It is not that while I am training I cannot help anybody, but I have to work on myself. I have to be the change. Without transforming myself, I cannot transform others.

We can train in compassion and in how we love people. We can train in how we see things and in how we react. We can also train our minds to be more calm. This is something everybody can learn.

Through reasoning, we can find that it is much better for myself and for the whole world if I am kinder and more compassionate. If I have lots of hatred, if I react with anger and greed, eventually I am the sufferer and I cause so much trouble for others. It is not good or useful for me to be that way. I need to train to be less negative, less angry and less jealous, and learn to be kinder, more compassionate and more loving. If I can do something helpful for others, then the one who is helped most is myself. Plus it also helps other people. So I must try to cultivate something that is good for me and good for everybody else. That is the motivation and the understanding.

Sometimes, people have the idea that "I am only doing things for others and it's not good for me. It is harming me." Sometimes, I have even heard people say, "I've been too compassionate, now it's time to look after myself."

I wonder how you would look after yourself without compassion? Being compassionate is actually more "looking after myself" than not being kind and not being loving and not being compassionate.

Of course, being compassionate doesn't mean that you are compelled to do things that you don't want to do, or are not prepared to do. You have to learn how to progress step by step. So therefore, I think we should talk about the first of Six Paramitas. This is the Paramita of Generosity, which is sometimes called the Paramita of Giving.

1
THE PARAMITA OF
Generosity

The Paramita of Generosity is first because our whole practice is inspired by wanting to help. We see lots of pain and suffering in ourselves and in other people, so we want to do something that is good and helpful for everybody.

Usually, the first things we think about giving are material things. So many beings in the world suffer because they don't have basic necessities like food, clothes and shelter. So, giving these is how we train. But this is about giving with joy, not giving as if you are forced to give.

Because if you feel forced you don't like it, you have resistance and then it is not real generosity. If somebody comes to ask for a donation, you want to lock up and hide somewhere. You feel as if somebody has taken a piece of your flesh. There is no necessity to give if you don't want to, or if you are not prepared for it. If you feel like that, then you should not give, because it will only make you less generous and even more resistant.

That is why it is said that if somebody asks

you for a cup of curry, put *lots* of chilli in it so they don't eat too much! I'm joking. If you have no problem giving a cup of curry, then give it and give it happily. Give it and be joyful. The training is that you do it as long as you can do it joyfully. You do it as long as you feel good and you have no regrets.

When you can give with more and more joy, you feel good because you feel you have done something useful. It is said that this is the best way to develop love for yourself, because if you help others you feel proud of yourself. Especially when you see their gratitude and the help that you have actually been able to give.

A few years ago I read an article about how researchers at Harvard Law School were astonished to find that people feel better when they spend their money on others rather than on themselves. That's not what we usually think. I was thinking that I would feel much better to spend on myself than on others. Although it would be good to spend on others, you know, it would be more positive if I did it for myself.

Maybe I have five pounds or something like that, so I buy an ice cream. But as soon as I finish eating, I feel maybe I shouldn't have that much ice cream. I won't feel any better tonight, I won't feel any better tomorrow, I may even feel a little bad. Now, if instead of eating the ice cream I gave it to somebody, or gave something that I know would be very helpful, perhaps I won't feel very good at the time, but that night when I think back, maybe I will be a little bit proud of myself. "You know, I really did something." Tomorrow also I might say, "Yesterday I did a great thing, I gave five pounds and I'm so good." Next year I might even remember, "Oh, yes, last year I did something good with my five pounds." Maybe I can be happy and proud of myself all my life, every time I remember, just with five pounds. So it made me happy, no? It made me much more proud of myself than just eating ice cream, which I would have actually regretted afterwards. So, if we think a little more deeply, if you are doing it joyfully, giving is actually good for us also and not just for other people.

There was a very rich man who used to come and listen when the Buddha was giving teachings. The man was rich, but he was not at all generous.

Sometimes Buddha spoke about how good it is to be generous and giving. So one day the man came up to Buddha and said, "You know, I like you. I like your teachings. I like being with you, but this generosity business is not for me. I don't want to be generous, it's not my thing. If I give anything for free it's like cutting off a piece of my own flesh."

Buddha said, "But you can train."

"No, I can't train."

Buddha said, "Do you mind giving to yourself?"

"No, of course not."

Then Buddha said, "Okay, in that case, do one thing. Take something valuable in your right hand, give it to your left hand and say, 'Take it!' And then give it back to your right hand and say, 'Take it!' Just do that exercise."

I think the man was a little curious. He went home and he took a big lump of gold (he had so many of them) and said, "Take it!" and gave it to his left hand. At first, he didn't feel so good, but he kept doing it again and again for some time. "Take it! Take it! Take it!" Then one day he thought, "Maybe it would be good to invite Buddha for lunch."

So he gave a lunch and Buddha came and gave a teaching. It all went very well and the man felt very good. Then he thought, "Why not invite the whole sangha?" So he made arrangements and invited the Buddha and all his monks and gave them food and drink. It was very nice and he felt very good. Then he became more and more generous. He opened hospitals and he made dharamsalas. A dharamsala is a kind of free hostel or hotel for travelers or people who need shelter for a short time. He built orphanages, he opened hospitals for the animals and he did so many things that he came to be known as Anathapindika, which means "Giver of Food To Those Who Have No Protection."

Once, Anathapindika wanted to give Buddha a kind of park for his Summer Retreat. He found an extremely nice forest with ponds and lawns and things like that. But the forest was owned by a prince, who didn't really like Buddha very much and when Anathapindika asked him to sell it, the prince quoted an unimaginably high price. Anathapindika just said "Okay" and gave him the money, and then he named the park Jetavana after the prince.

When the prince heard this, he was totally surprised. "What kind of person is this?" he thought. "I quoted a price that nobody could pay, but he didn't even bargain. He just gave me the money and then he actually gave my name to the forest. This is something special. There must be something good going on there." So he came and listened to the Buddha's teachings and then he also became his student and did many good things.

So, the training has to be like that. Step by step. No compulsion. If you have resistance to it, or if you feel regret, then don't do it at that time.

Generosity is not only about giving material things, but also about giving protection, guidance and kindness. Anything that I want, everybody else wants also. A little smile, or a nice word. Sometimes appreciation is much more valuable to somebody than being given lots of material things. Sometimes we are too stingy with appreciation. We do not fully praise somebody who has good qualities, or who is doing something good. Why not? I think many people are not able to express their love, and so there are lots of misunderstandings and things like that.

The more your generosity can grow step by step, then the more your resistance to giving diminishes. Perhaps that resistance is a form of clinging, or attachment. Sometimes it is said that the highest form of generosity is having no attachment, because the less you are attached, the more openhearted you are.

Our attachment is not only to material things. We can be very attached to our name, our fame, our identities and things like that, and then we are not able to share.

«In Tibetan Buddhism, we have a practice called Mandala Offering.»

If I do something, then I feel that *I* should get the credit, or that I should not give credit to others. Slowly, slowly, as we become more generous, we actually become much happier, freer and lighter. The most important thing is that we are not clinging so much.

Sometimes we are more attached to things we do not have than to the things we have. In Tibetan Buddhism we have a practice called Mandala Offering, which is an exercise in giving mind-created gifts. We imagine all kinds of positive things and we say, "I give it there, I dedicate it." We also give our positive karma. At the beginning of the practice I say, "I want to do this so that it will be good not only for me, but for everybody." Then at the end of the practice I say, "Whatever good result, whatever good karma, whatever positive things come out of these positive actions -and not only the positive actions that I do now, but all the positive actions I have done before and that I will be doing in the future- all of them together I want to dedicate. I want to give to *every* being, so that everyone can enjoy the result of this positive action." When I say this deeply and genuinely, I am not only giving something material, I am also giving the *causes* of these positive things.

This exercise of offering not only little things, but my positive everything as well as my positive karma and the causes of future positive things, is an exercise of the mind. Maybe I don't get anything at the moment, but it's a big exercise for me that I do not hold on, that I do not cling or have too much attachment to things. If I am not attached to even my positive karma, then I will not be attached to anything that I have around me. When I am not attached, I am not worried about them, and if I am not worried about them, then I am not caught, or not engaged with attachment to anything.

If we cannot give, or if we feel that we do not have very much, we do this exercise of generosity in our minds, and then slowly, slowly we can give a little bit more.

«If we can not give, we do this exercise of generosity in our mind.»

Sometimes we visualize the most magnificent gifts of palaces and universes with every possible kind of positive thing in them. We visualize countless offerings coming from our hearts to everybody throughout space. So if in my imagination I give palaces and all these great things, then to give a cup of curry is not such a big deal! So, it's like that. That's the training.

Questioner: Could you say a little more about being attached to things that you don't have, please?

Rinpoche: Well, you can be attached to anything. Like the nice garden here, or even that nice flower. Now, saying this is a nice flower and enjoying it is not a problem, but usually we don't stop there. Next is, "I wish I had it", then, "How can I get it?" and then the problems begin. "Who does it belong to?" and I make it so you have to give it to me, even if you don't want to. And now, more problems. How to carry it on my plane? Now what will happen to my flower? You can be very attached to things. You like something, but you don't have it, and then you feel, "I have nothing, because I don't have this garden, I don't have this palace, I don't have this flower." So you can feel like you have nothing, even if you have lots of things.

Questioner: Rinpoche, I find it hard to get my mind around the idea of imagining giving huge palaces and wealth and so on when I don't have them. I can't imagine having a convincing feeling of giving all those things.

Rinpoche: Actually, even when we have them, in a way we are imagining having them. Can we really own anything? Can we take it when we die? If I say I own this flower, only my mind says I own this flower, but actually this flower will grow old. Maybe somebody will take care of it, or maybe somebody won't take care of it and it will wither and die. So, what did I own? It was just a concept.

A man died and then an angel came and said, "Let's go."

And the man says, "Where? I don't want to go."

"But you are dead."

"I don't want to die, I have so many things to do. I have so many plans."

"That doesn't matter, you are dead."

The angel is carrying a box and the man is curious. He says, "What's in that box?"

"It's yours."

The man becomes more curious. "What, like my clothing and my belongings?"

«So the angel opens the box...»

"No, no, no. Those are from the earth. You have nothing like that. You cannot carry property and things like that with you."

"Then maybe they are like my talents and things like that"

"No, you got those talents through circumstances. They're not yours, they're finished."

"Okay, maybe it's my love and my relationships and things like that."

"No, they don't belong to you. They belonged to your heart. It's finished."

"Maybe it's my soul."

"No, your soul never belonged to you, it belonged to me."

Then the man says, "What is it then? What is in that box?"

"You want to look?"

"Yes"

So the angel opens the box and it is totally empty.

The man says, "Is there nothing that belongs to me?"

"No, nothing belongs to you."

"But then what did I have? What did I have?"

The angel says, "You had your moments. Those moments were yours and you wasted your moments."

So it's a little bit like that. This very moment is kind of ours. We can do whatever we want with that and then it's gone. Life is full of moments, but what do we have, actually? We don't have anything. We can't really own anything, but we think we do. So if we can think we own lots of things when we really cannot, why can't we imagine we own more?

There are two ways of looking at how rich you are. The materialistic way is about how many things you have, but from the spiritual point of view being rich is about how satisfied and content you are. You can be a millionaire and yet be very poor if you are greedy and think you need more. So, if I am satisfied and content I am very rich, but if I am discontented and dissatisfied I am very poor because I don't have enough.

There is a story from Buddha's time about a poor lady who found a big gold coin. So she goes to the Buddha and says, "I found this special gold coin, but I don't want to keep it. I want to give it to the most needy one. Can you advise me who to give it to?"

Buddha names the richest man in town and says, "Maybe you should give it to him."

She is not convinced, but she is very devoted to Buddha, so she goes to the man's house and when he comes to the door she says, "I have a gold coin and I want to give it to the one who is the most needy. Buddha gave me your name, but I really don't think I've come to the right place. I think you are not the one."

And the man looks at this gold coin and says, "Oh, Buddha is absolutely right. I have nine hundred and ninety-nine of these and I am desperately looking for one so that it becomes a thousand." So you see, if you have more it doesn't mean that you are satisfied and don't need more.

«Buddha named the richest man in town and said, «Maybe you should give it to him.»»

Questioner: My question is, when we give sometimes, why do we feel so tired afterwards? Why do we feel depleted?

Rinpoche: I think even if we are not giving anything, most of the time we're tired because there are lots of things going on in our minds. We are busy worrying about things and planning things and there are lots of things so we are usually tired. Of course, when you do something that makes you happy and joyful, then you don't get tired. When you do something which is like a duty you feel tired. So I think it is to do with how we see things. It's also possible that when we give time to others, maybe we kind of think, "Oh, I have to do something for others. I want to give this time, but it's not so enjoyable." People can get tired by doing things and not doing things as well as by talking and thinking. Sometimes if you don't drink water, you get tired. I found that if I drink two or three glasses of water, immediately all my tiredness goes away. So, drink some water.

Questioner: I read a story that involves generosity. A person cuts off his arm and is told, "Oh, your left arm's no good to me, I need your right one," but then he couldn't cut that off because he had already cut off the left one. The story seemed to be saying that the man was trying to give before he had achieved a certain level of realisation. Is there any kind of guidance in terms of our practice before we really are able to effortlessly practice generosity, please?

Rinpoche: Generally it is said that if you understand that something is good for you and for others, then there's no reason why you should not do it. If it's neither good for you nor for others, then why would you do it? If it's good for yourself and it doesn't harm others, then maybe you can do it. If it is a little bit good for you, but more harmful to others, maybe there is something else you can do. If it's good for others but not so good for you, then you have to see how bad it is for me and how good it is for others. If it's only a little good for others and quite bad for you there's no need to do anything. But if it is very good for others and a little bit bad for you, then you have to think about whether you are okay with that or not. If you have no regrets, then you can do it. But if you are not prepared and you know you will regret it afterwards, then you don't need to do it. That's the general understanding.

I think the story you may have read is about one of the former lives of Shariputra, one of the two main students of the Buddha. It is said that he became a very enthusiastic bodhisattva. Too enthusiastic, in a way. He proclaimed, "I never say no to anybody. I gave up saying no. If anybody wants anything from me, just ask and I give." So of course lots of people came, but as he was a rich man he went on giving everything that they asked for. It went on and on for years and then one day a very bad kind of person came and said, "Is it true that you don't say no to anything and you give whatever anybody asks?"

"Yes, I am a bodhisattva. Anything you want, tell me. If I have it, I give it."

Then the man said, "Can you give me your right hand, please."

Sharipurtra had no hesitation. He just took a sword and cut off his right hand and gave it to the man. But then this person said, "How can I accept something that is given to me with the left hand?" You know, usually in India, it's not considered good to give anything with your left hand.

So now, what happens to Sharipurtra's mind? He's not so accepting now. He says, "No more of this bodhisattva business. Why should anybody try to help these people who are so ungrateful?" So one should start with something that you can do joyfully and then, if it really helps lots of beings in a big way and you have absolutely no regrets, at *that* point you may give your life, but not until then. So this is the idea. It is not just about giving, but giving to benefit others.

Questioner: Rinpoche, there was a request from Lama Chodrak to collect a hundred million *OM MANI PEME HUNG* recitations. He says that His Holiness Karmapa's Kagyu Monlam is only a few days long and that there won't be time to recite 100,000,000 mantras, so the request is to collect recitations and send the number you have completed by email. Of course, it would be best to count mantras while you're doing the Chenrezig sadhana, but if you can't do that, you say the mantra and concentrate on generating compassion for all beings. All the recitations will be dedicated to world peace and harmony. Everyone who participates will collect merit equal to the full 100,000,000 recitations.

Rinpoche: You know, from the Buddhist point of view, it is said that when lots of people do something together, it has a more powerful consequence. If all of us together do something bad, like kill a chicken, then it's not that we will get just one per cent of the bad effect, but that each one of us will have the negative karma of killing a chicken. However, if all of us together do one big thing, then each of us will have the positive karma of doing that whole thing. So if everybody together contributes mantras, it means that when it's done, it's like each one has completed 100,000,000 mantras.

2
THE PARAMITA OF
Shila / Discipline

The second Paramita is the Paramita of Shila, which means "good conduct" in Sanskrit. Sometimes it is also translated as "discipline" or "ethics."

I think many people have a problem about ethics, especially if they feel that they are being *told* to do something or told *not* to do something. I also have that attitude. If somebody tells me, "You have to do that," I think, "Why should I?" And if somebody tells me, "You cannot do that," then I want to do it. Maybe that is human nature.

They say there is an area in Africa that is completely desert. Only one tribe of people lives there because only they know how to get water. Nobody lives in this whole area except this remote tribe and a few monkeys. The people have a method for getting water from the monkeys and this is how they do it. First they find a monkey and then they just kind of sit nearby and do nothing. The monkey thinks that the human is going to kill him, but the man isn't even moving, he is just sitting there.

So after a few days, the monkey is quite calm and comes a little bit nearer. Then the man digs a little hole, just as big as a monkey can put his hand in, and inside that hole he puts a stone. The monkey looks and says, "What's in this hole? Maybe there's something nice." And then he says, "No, no, I shouldn't go near it. Human beings are always bad. There's always some trick."

But then he gets curious, "What is there?" So he comes nearer, and nearer, "No, no, I shouldn't do that." But there seems to be nothing wrong so he puts his hand in a little bit. Nothing happens, so he puts his hand in a little more. Nothing happens, so he becomes more and more courageous and more and more curious. He puts his hand in completely and then he feels this stone. So he takes hold of it and tries to bring his hand out, but he cannot because now he has made a fist. Then he panics and his fist gets even tighter. And that's when the man catches the monkey. He ties him to a rope and ties the other end to a rock.

«He takes hold of it and tries to bring his hand out,
but he cannot because now he made a fist.»

Shila / Discipline

The monkey says, "I *knew* it! Human beings are always like that. What a fool I am. I shouldn't have gone near it."

Now the man puts down a plate with lots of salt and again the monkey wants to see and wants to touch. He says, "No, I shouldn't," but then he touches it and he likes the taste. He says, "No, I shouldn't eat it," but he eats all the salt and now he is so thirsty that he tries to run away. And the man knows exactly when to free him. When the monkey is totally desperate for water the man lets him go and then follows him directly to the rocks where the water is found.

So, we are a little bit like that monkey. Sometimes our emotions are so strong that we cannot control them even though we know they cause harm. We have to find out why we are like that. What actions bring problems, pain and suffering to ourselves and others, and what actions bring benefit and positive things? If we can be clearer about that, we can learn to do more of what is helpful and beneficial and train ourselves to do less of what is harmful.

Shila / Discipline

This is the basis of understanding the actions of body, speech and mind.

It is very important to understand that our actions of body and speech are under the control of the mind. If we react with too much anger and hatred, greed or jealousy, then the actions that result from that are usually not only harmful to ourselves, but harmful to others also. Sometimes our emotions are so strong that, like the monkey, we have to do something even if we know that this action is not good. According to the Buddhist way, we need meditation because if we have a method to work on our emotions and reactions, then our minds become more flexible and more tamed, and we can do more of what we know is good and less of what we know is harmful.

As with the generosity practice, we are aiming not to be so attached to things, so that becomes the basis of the discipline. The less we are attached to our emotions and to our things, the more we can perceive what is good to do and what is not good to do and then act on that.

As many of you know, in Buddhism, all the practices come down to three trainings:

- The training of how we act, which is the training of our conduct.
- The training of wisdom, which is the training of how to see, clearly and directly, the nature of the way things really are.
- And then the training of mind, which is meditation.

In the training of conduct, we sometimes take precepts. For example, if you see very clearly that an action is very bad to do and you take a precept, it means that you make a promise to yourself that you are not going to do this. "I'm not going to kill," or something like that.

In Buddhism, we talk about three kinds of precepts: Vinaya precepts, Bodhisattva precepts and Vajrayana precepts. Vinaya precepts are common to Theravada, Mahayana and Vajrayana Buddhism. There is no real difference between them.

Sometimes people say, "Oh, in some

schools of Tibetan Buddhism, the monks can marry." That is a wrong perception. If they have taken the Vinaya vows, then they have taken Vinaya vows and they cannot marry. If they have *not* taken Vinaya vows, they can still be practitioners of dharma, but they are not monks. They have other precepts, but not Vinaya precepts. This is important to understand because there can be a lot of misunderstanding.

If you look into the Vinaya precepts, you will always find an emphasis on *not* doing this and *not* doing that. They are basically about not harming, about refraining from doing something bad. For example, in the five precepts of householders, the main precept is not killing a human being or a human being to be. Then there's not stealing, not telling lies, not committing sexual misconduct and not getting intoxicated and things like that. If you want to, you can take one of the five precepts. Or you can take two, or three or four. If you want to take all five, you can take all five.

There is also a practice which Buddha

very much encouraged: the practice of taking precepts for one day. He said so many good things about that. He said that if you take the eight precepts[1] for one day, then you will never be born into the lower realms.

If you practice Buddhism, there is nothing like you have to do *all* these things. Maybe I shouldn't say this because then you may only want to do the smallest thing! But I think it is important to understand that you can start at the simplest, most easy level. I like that approach. It is like a training. We train to reduce negative deeds of our body, speech and mind as much as possible and then we also increase positive deeds as much as possible.

So, from the Buddhist point of view, discipline means *knowing* what actions are positive or negative. Positive means something that benefits myself and others now and in the long run. Something that brings pain and suffering for myself and others now and in the long run is called negative. Once we understand, then we say okay, this is not good for me and not good for others, so, I *allow* myself not to do it. And if other actions are good for myself and others, then I *allow* myself to do them.

Sometimes, life is much easier once you have made this clear decision, because many times the problem is, "Should I do it or should I not do it?"

When I was very young we had to wake up a little bit before the first session, which was at four o'clock. Many times I had a headache. My teacher slept in the same room, so every time I said "I have a headache," he said, "Okay it doesn't matter, you sleep." But I think he knew very well that I didn't really have a headache. One day he said, "You know, in the morning when the gong rings, if you think about whether you should get up or not, then you will not be able to get up." He said, "You should not think. Especially, you should never roll over in the bed, because once you roll over you won't want to get up." This is much easier, because you don't have to decide, "Do I want to do this or do I not want to do this?" When the gong rings you just get up, and once you're up it's actually much nicer. You don't have to tell a lie, because one lie leads to another and after some time, "Oh, he's having a headache all the time, bring the doctor," and he might give me a very, very bitter pill. Tibetan pills are very bitter, you know!

So, discipline is just making a decision about knowing what is good and then without too much thinking, allowing yourself to follow that decision. That is why making a commitment or taking a precept is important because once I make that decision, then I don't have to think again and again and again. All these things are a training.

A bodhisattva's ethics, or precepts, include the precepts of the Vinaya. The Six Paramitas is actually the Bodhisattva's ethics and the Six Paramitas is also the training. So the understanding is that the more you train to do less negative things, the more you don't want to do them, and the more you don't need to do them. So, that becomes your habit, and after some time it is not difficult. You actually like it much more because it is better for you and better for others.

But to begin with, it is necessary to make a clear decision based on knowing the pros and cons of any action. Sometimes, it is even said that this decision can affect our habitual tendencies in life after life.

There is a difference between just not doing negative things, and taking a precept. If you just *happen* not to do something negative, there is always the possibility that you will do it because you have not decided totally against it. But if you make a decision and you take a precept not to do it, then you have ruled out that action. You made a complete decision. That is why it has more effect on your habitual tendency.

There was a monk during the time of Buddha, an arhat called Katyana. He traveled long distances alone, so the accounts of his travels are very interesting. Once, he was in a desert area where he saw a very strange man. The whole day, this man was being bitten and mauled by four ferocious dogs, so he was in great pain. However, as soon as night came, the four dogs turned into beautiful girls, who were worshipping him the whole night.

Katyana was very surprised and asked, "What's going on with you? This is so strange." The man explained that in his previous life he was a butcher and he was killing animals. Then one day he met a monk who spoke about the negative karma of killing.

The man said, "I cannot *not* kill. I'm a butcher by profession. If I don't kill animals I won't earn any money and cannot support my family. What can I do?"

The monk said, "Do you butcher animals at night?"

"No, at night I go to bed."

"Why don't you make a precept, a promise that you will not kill any animals during the night?"

«He is in a hell realm in the daytime,
but at night he has no problem!»

The man said, "That I can do. There's no problem because I don't kill any animals at night anyway." So he made this promise not to kill any animals at night and because of this, he is in a hell realm in the daytime, but at night he has no problem! This story illustrates that when one makes a precept, then it is much stronger in you, because you cut off the possibility of doing that action.

We usually talk about three Shilas. The first Shila is abstaining from doing negative things, which is regarded as a very positive thing. The second is to increase positive actions with joy and understanding. In this way, your habitual tendency to do positive actions will be increased. Like working on your generosity, for example, or doing actions that would be useful for you and for everybody- like the Six Paramitas. And then third is one of the most positive: the action of helping others.

Most people who are intelligent and good and strong do not need much help. The people who need help are those who are not in a good way, who have bad habits, who don't understand

and who are addicted in different ways. To be able to help them is not easy. I think it is very, very important to understand that right from the beginning. It is also not certain whether the help really benefits or not, because the benefit does not depend on your action alone. How the help is received depends on many circumstances, so it is not enough that you do the right thing. When we try to help someone, we should be very clear that it might *not* help.

Many people such as healers, psychologists or therapists can get burnt out very easily. And I see why. They try very hard, and if they don't have 100% positive results they feel responsible. If you take it like that, you get exhausted. You get overwhelmed and you get burnt out. Therefore, helping should be done with patience, thinking, "I will do my best. I will do whatever I can, but whatever result comes, I have to accept it."

When we talk about helping we are talking about four things. The first is generosity. One must have the willingness and generosity of a helping attitude. You are really concerned about the people you want to help and not too concerned about what people will say, or whether you will be appreciated or not. Because if you are too concerned about yourself, then you can become too emotional and too hurt. Most of the time, you know, people don't necessarily appreciate it. Some people can be very ungracious.

I have a story to illustrate this. It is supposed to be one of the Ten Jatakas, which are about the ten lives of the Buddha before he became Buddha.

The Bodhisattva was born as an extraordinary white elephant. His tusks were golden and his lips were like petals. He was called All Good and he was extremely beautiful and gracious, powerful and kind. Of course, all the elephants followed him and he became the king of all the animals. He ruled a big elephant group and wherever he went, they went there too. So he said, "Now, I want to go away because this is becoming too much. Please, let me alone, it's not good for you." Then the elephant went alone into the jungle.

One day, a man got lost deep in the forest. He tried everything, but couldn't find the way out. He was very frightened, crying and shouting, "I'm going to die. Please, somebody help me." There were no people around for a great distance, but the elephant heard him and came. As soon as the man saw this big elephant, he was frightened and ran. And when he ran, the elephant stopped. The man stopped running and the elephant slowly came towards him. Again the man ran, but then he realised that the elephant didn't intend to harm him, so he didn't run any more.

The elephant came near and said, "What's wrong with you? You are crying for help." And the man said, "Well, I'm totally lost and I'm afraid. I'm hungry and thirsty. Maybe I'll die."

The elephant said, "Don't worry, I'll help you." He gave the man fruits and water and then lifted him onto his back and took him to the edge of the forest where he could find people. "Now, I leave you here," the elephant said. "Go home, but please don't tell anybody about me."

So the man went home to Varanasi and there he found people selling elephant tusks at a very high price. He knew how good and how compassionate this elephant was and he thought, "You know, if I go back and ask for his tusk, I think he will give it." So he took a saw and went back to the jungle. And when the man met the elephant he said, "Oh I'm so glad to meet you. I went home, but my children are hungry." Then he was crying and said, "We are so desperate and we are so poor. I and all my children are going to die of hunger, but if you can give a little bit of your tusk, maybe we can survive."

The elephant said, "Okay. Cut a little bit off my tusk and take it. No problem. But do you have something to cut it?"

"Yes!" So the man cut a little bit of the tusk and then he went off and sold it.

After a few days he came back again crying, "Can you give..." So the elephant gave another piece. And it was like this every time the man came.

By now there is hardly any tusk left,

but yet again the man comes back and says, "Ah, give me the rest of your tusk. You don't need it now, this tusk is hardly a tusk. So, I take everything."

The elephant was compassionate and said, "Okay, take everything."

So the man cut not only the tusk, but went deep inside and cut the flesh. Right from the bottom he took it. He knew he didn't need to come back any more, so he didn't even thank the elephant, who was standing there bleeding and suffering from all the pain. He just left.

The elephant took it nicely, but the earth could not take any more. When the man came a little bit away from the forest, the earth shook. It shook so violently that it split into two and the man fell into it. But when the elephant died, he went straight to the Heaven of the Thirty-Three and became the Buddha.

So human beings can be a little bit like that, you know. The more you give, the more they want. I think it is important to know that.

Sometimes people say, "People want to take advantage of me!" But if you think that people will never take advantage then you don't understand human beings. If some people *don't* take advantage you have to be extremely grateful. Most people want to take advantage, but it's up to us how much we allow them to take. It's not like, "I don't want to help any more because they just want to take advantage." I know people will take advantage, but I still want to help as much as I can.

Then secondly, your speech is very important. Many times when we help, we can be a little bit proud and arrogant.

Being kind and respectful is sometimes more helpful than the actual thing you do. Everything is about the mind and about how you feel, so if you can make this person feel good, respected and loved, then that is very important.

So, first is generosity, second is being mindful about how you speak, and third is about what the person needs and not about what *I* want to do.

«If you are kind and respectful, that is sometimes more helpful than the actual thing you do.»

Many times, we think we know what people need, and then even if they don't want it we kind of impose it on them. Many times they don't use it well, because they don't know how to use it most probably. Then it doesn't benefit them and we get annoyed: "I spent so much time and effort and money on this. Why do you waste all these things?"

I saw this many times. Mrs Freda Bedi, a very nice, good English lady who started the Young Lamas School for Tulkus where I studied, was also my English teacher. One Christmas, her gift to me was that any time I spoke in English and made a mistake, she would immediately correct me. I can't open my mouth, but she is there! But it was so useful, you know. Then she invited forty young girls between the ages of fourteen and sixteen to see whether they wanted to become nuns, so we were all together for one winter. She was teaching me English while she was building a nunnery. After that, I was with her for about six months visiting Tibetan settlements, which were not established by the Tibetan

Government. Khampas always want to be independent. "We don't want any help from the Tibetan Government. We want to do it ourselves." So she used to visit them and I was translating for her. Sometimes it was so funny. People want to help, but if the people don't want that, there is such a tussle going on! That is one important thing; it's not about what I want or what I think, but what they want and what they need.

So these are the four main kinds of training on how to help people: Generosity, how to use your language, what people need, and then living or acting in accordance with the people that you want to help. That is part of discipline and ethics also.

Mahatma Gandhi was a highly educated barrister, but he went back to India and actually became one of the people. He put on a loincloth, the very thing that untouchable, low caste people wear. He wore the same clothes, he lived in the same places, did the same things and ate the same food. And then he became so influential that when he began the Quit India Movement, all the people came, because he was living like one of them.

So, trying to abstain from doing negative things, trying to increase positive actions, and then training in how to properly help people. These three trainings constitute the Paramita of Shila.

«Mahatma Ghandi was a highly educated barrister, but he went back to India and became one of the people.»

Questioner: Rinpoche, I wondered what is the correct way to understand the story you told about the beautiful white elephant. Because when the earth opened up and the man who had stolen the elephant's tusks fell in, I noticed that I was pleased. Maybe that's not quite right.

Rinpoche: Well, that is the Jataka story. I don't know whether you should feel pleased or displeased. There are so many stories of this kind. I'm sure you know all of these stories teach us something. People can be very ungrateful and greedy. And if you are very ungrateful and very greedy you cause a lot of harm to others, but eventually you cause more harm to yourself. I think that's the moral of the story.

Questioner: I suppose the western way of dealing with bad behavior is a more psychotherapeutic approach, which takes the unconscious into account. I wonder about certain behaviors, which could perhaps be reactions or chemistry, and I'm not sure if they can be abstained from or abolished with one act of decision.

Rinpoche: From the Buddhist point of view, it is believed that we can change this habitual tendency to react according to what we have been doing all along. It is difficult because it is habitual, but it can be changed through understanding why you should do it and why you should not do it, and through repetition again and again. Say, for instance, I feel guilty, or I feel fear, or I am worried. All these things are coming from a deep level of my unconscious mind and so I almost automatically react in that way. But if you deeply understand that that way of reacting is not necessary, or good, or useful, then when you behave like that, you understand that you reacted out of habit. When your consciousness catches it and says, no, it's not necessary, we can sometimes let go of it more easily. So, when we can do it again and again, slowly, slowly, slowly, it can change.

There is a story about a shepherd who

was looking after his sheep somewhere in the Himalayas. Near his place there was a cave and in this cave there lived a very highly attained meditator who was so famous that people used to come from far and wide to receive teachings from him. One day, the shepherd thought, "I must also go and try to get some instructions." So he went and said, "I am just a shepherd. I am totally ignorant and illiterate and I know nothing. Please can you give me some instructions."

So the master said, "Okay, I can give you instructions, but can you make two little bags?"

"Oh, that's no problem."

So he went and made two little bags and then the master said, "Okay, now you go and fill these bags, one with black pebbles and one with white pebbles." So the shepherd filled one with black pebbles and one with white pebbles and back he came.

Then the master said, "Okay, now go and sit where you usually sit under that rock and do nothing, but just see what happens to your mind.

If a positive thought comes, a good thought, a benevolent thought, a helping thought, you take out a white pebble and put it to your right side. When a negative thought comes, like anger or wanting to harm, you take out a black pebble and put it on the left. Just do that."

So the shepherd is sitting there and seeing what is coming up. One black pebble, two black pebbles, three black pebbles. So he went back and said, "I think there's something wrong. I have used only two or three white pebbles, but the black pebbles are all gone."

The Master says, "You don't have to worry about that. Put all the pebbles in your bags and go away and do nothing, just as I said. Less white doesn't matter. You just do it. It's like a game."

So every day, the shepherd is sitting there, seeing what is coming up. And then slowly, slowly, his black pebbles are reducing and the white pebbles are increasing, although he is not doing anything consciously. So like that he was changing, and after a long time, he had only white pebbles. So that's the method. You become a little bit aware, but there is no need to struggle, no need to punish, no need to order, no need to do anything but just become aware of what is going on, and through that, slowly, slowly, you kind of change your level of your consciousness.

Questioner: When mindfulness is taught in the West, they often talk about watching your thoughts and not getting caught up in them, but there is nothing about discernment between what thoughts might be positive and beneficial for yourself and others. It occurs to me that ethics isn't included in the material that is taught. When you just said about how awareness can, of its own nature, kind of tip the balance, would that be in terms of mindfulness? Is just being aware enough?

Rinpoche: Well, this style of teaching mindfulness was started in America by Jon Kabat-Zinn and others. I met them. They are all actually Buddhist teachers. Although they don't deny that this is coming from Buddhist sources, they tried to be very secular and take away all spiritual, religious terminologies so that anybody, from any background, can do it. And it has its place, that is why it was successful. Now, mindfulness is used by everybody. The CIA wanted it. The army wanted it. Then, people said that if the army used meditation that they would become very good sharpshooters and things like that. Of course, it's not really designed to make sharpshooters, but it will help. Techniques can be used in this or that way or whatever, so maybe it is better to base them on compassion and empathy right from the beginning. I think these things are happening slowly. The Google headquarters of Europe in Ireland invited me. I didn't understand why, but it seems they have invited all kinds of meditators and spiritual people. They have a really good book called "Searching Inside Yourself." Not googling outside, but googling inside!

But I was also thinking that maybe this is my businessman side talking. You know, my family used to think that I would be a good businessman if I didn't become a Lama because I supported my family from my childhood. I bought a very old car for 60,000 Rupees and ran it as a business. I went to see the wife of the Chief Minister, who was a colleague of mine, and asked her to give me a license. So for many years we were living on this taxi. Then I ran a printing press on my own for about fifteen years. I did the business side, getting jobs, doing all the quotations, accounting, book-keeping, selling, employment, proofreading, everything.

There is a tendency among those who have been practising meditation for a long time to see mindfulness as being a bit superficial and watered down and so they don't take part in it. Then people who know nothing about Buddhism or meditation become experts in mind training, charging lots of money from everybody, while Buddhists, whose pockets are not so full, don't take advantage of this great opportunity! They have been training for so long, trying to learn meditation for many years, so they would be better than anybody else to teach mindfulness, but they are not doing it. It is just poor business sense, I think! So I am trying to encourage Buddhist meditators to go into it and take over and charge lots of money and become rich!

Questioner: Often when I am in dharma circles, I feel I am defending mindfulness and when I'm in a clinical setting, I feel I'm defending dharma. I understand why there's a debate. However, in the Trust I work in, two or three top clinical psychologists and dharma practitioners were very instrumental in bringing in mindfulness and compassion. I share the concerns you mention, but I've seen evidence of people just beginning a little path and sowing seeds of more self-kindness and less suffering. I'm thinking it's a very positive thing, but we all need to be careful around what it is we're doing, and how skilled we are in it, as well as our own practice. And you're quite right, there are people doing short mindfulness courses who are then setting themselves up to teach independently. But I feel very inspired and I feel different now after hearing your words.

Rinpoche: I think it should be like you describe how it is at your workplace. His Holiness, the Dalai Lama is working hard on bringing in secular ethics based on compassion, but not based on any particular philosophy or religion. That would be very good, because it doesn't necessarily belong to one kind of religion or one section of people. And then it could actually help the world become a little bit more ethical, because the main problem of the world, the wars and the environment, is actually because of the lack of ethics, no? People are not thinking about how their actions are affecting other people, or the future, or the world. They're only thinking about how to get more money. And corporate ethics is considered the best! It's very dangerous.

Questioner: Ethics seems to be an awareness practice because it forces us to be more compassionate with ourselves and then more compassionate with others. In life, almost inevitably you break the precepts, so there is a moral dilemma. I'm wondering, what would you say about what to do when one has broken the precepts, even though you've tried your very best?

Rinpoche: Generally, you try to be clear about what kind of precepts you take. The precept of not killing is not about not killing anything; it is about not killing human beings and human beings to be. I think the Buddha knew that if you are a householder or a cattle farmer or have to work in the fields, it may not be possible not to kill. Of course you should try not to kill, but that is not part of the precept. This is important to understand. I have seen some people who made this precept much stricter, saying not to kill any animals, or indeed, any beings. That is very good, but whether it is practically possible or not, is another matter.

Shila / Discipline

It is also said that what we call negative deeds, especially of body and speech, have to be seen in terms of ultimate consequences. If something is done in order to prevent something more negative, then to do a negative deed is sometimes regarded as positive. That is important, but it is not good to say too much about this, because our ego is very intelligent and it can always find an excuse. The history of mankind is basically a story of wars and all these wars were supposed to be fought for some good reason. But actually, it is very easy to say "I'm doing it for a good cause." That's why I think it is a little bit dangerous.

Once, a great master, a Geshe, is supposed to have said to Atisha Dipankara, "I am practicing in retreat in a remote cave. If I break one of my precepts, what should I do?" The answer is very interesting, but maybe one should not talk too much about it. Atisha said, "If you break a precept, you go to Samye monastery and announce that you have broken that vow. Then you go to Tanduk, another monastery, and you say, I have broken my vow.

«And then you go back to your cave and act as if you have never broken anything.»

Then you go to Lhasa, and there also you say that you have broken that vow. And then you go back to your cave and act as if you have never broken anything."

3
THE PARAMITA OF
Patience

The third Paramita is the Paramita of Patience. There are three kinds of patience. One is a bit like forbearance, like being able to forbear hardship. You encounter something difficult and then you kind of lose heart and cannot go forward. So, not becoming overwhelmed like that is one kind of patience. This is very important because if we want to do something big or achieve something significant, if we have no patience, we will give up and then we can never achieve anything. This kind of patience is about being prepared for difficulties, hindrances and obstacles along the way.

If I want to transform myself and change my way of experiencing, then I need to change my habits. And changing habits is not easy because I have been doing these things all the time. Some negative habits become strong addictions, so if I want to become a better person I need to be free from these addictions. If I don't have patience when these problems arise, then I will not be able to transform myself.

We need to accept how difficult it will be. We need to be clear about how hard it is to change our habits and our emotions and our way of doing things. When we have that kind of clarity, when we *know* this, and are prepared for it, then when the obstacles come, we say, "Okay, this is normal, this is the way it is. I didn't expect it to be easier."

But if we expected it to be too easy, "There's no problem, you know, I just do ten minutes meditation and next year I will be enlightened." Then, when you don't get enlightened next year you say, "What's wrong with this thing? It's not working." Or you say, "What's wrong with *me*? I am no good."

That is why this first type of patience is very important. We need to understand that making a big difference is not easy and that forbearance is necessary, as well as not expecting too much result. Otherwise we are easily frustrated and overwhelmed, and then it is not possible to move forward.

«If you have to go on a long journey, you have to know how long it will take, how difficult the journey is and what the dangers are.»

If you have to go on a long journey, you have to know how long it will take, how difficult the journey is going to be and what the dangers are. If you clearly understand the difficulties, then you don't kind of rush in, but go with a certain kind of preparedness, and if everything doesn't come together it is okay, you know things are like that. So that is the first kind of patience.

The second kind of patience is about not being overpowered by hatred and anger. This kind of patience is regarded as being very important. From the Buddhist point of view, anger, which brings malevolent thoughts followed by hatred, is regarded as the most negative strong emotion.

In Buddhist terms, we describe three, or sometimes five main mind poisons. The first group of mind poisons, or kleshas, are anger, hatred and malevolent feelings. The second group is greed, attachment, too much clinging and too much desire. The third is confusion, ignorance and lack of clarity. Sometimes, two more groups are added: jealousy and envy and then, pride and arrogance.

Jealousy and envy are regarded as a combination of too much attachment and too much anger. Aversion and attachment together at the same time create jealousy. For example, "I like this, but I don't like somebody having this." Arrogance and pride are regarded as a combination of ignorance and attachment. I have too much attachment to myself and I don't know that I don't know, so I think I know everything, or something like that. So, there can be three or five of these destructive mind poisons.

There are some differences. For example, they say that although attachment brings pain and suffering, there can be some good things about it also. However, anger and especially hatred are regarded as having nothing good at all. Anger is regarded as absolutely the strongest, most harmful emotion. When you are angry and upset, it burns yourself as well as causing harm to the people for whom you have hatred. It is also harmful to everybody around the person who has so much hatred. So, it's not good for anybody, now or in the long run.

« When you have this anger and this hatred, you cannot wait. You have to treat it like a poisonous snake falling into your lap or as if your hair is on fire. »

Therefore, when you have this anger and this hatred, you cannot wait. You have to treat it like a poisonous snake falling into your lap or as if your hair is on fire. If your hair catches fire, you don't call the fireman and say, "Hello, my hair is on fire!" You just *do* something. Because if hatred catches you, you will do something terrible to yourself and to others. This is the understanding. If you act out of anger the people who hate you will hate even more and then *you* will hate more, and then they'll do something to you and then you become more hateful. Hatred begets hatred. It goes on and on and there is no end to it.

Anger comes as if it is something good for you, so you need to catch it with wisdom. All these negative emotions first arise as if to help you, "Oh poor you, you have been wronged. Why don't you get angry? You have the right to be angry." "*Yes*, I have the right to be angry! I must be angry," and then you say or do something that hurts somebody.

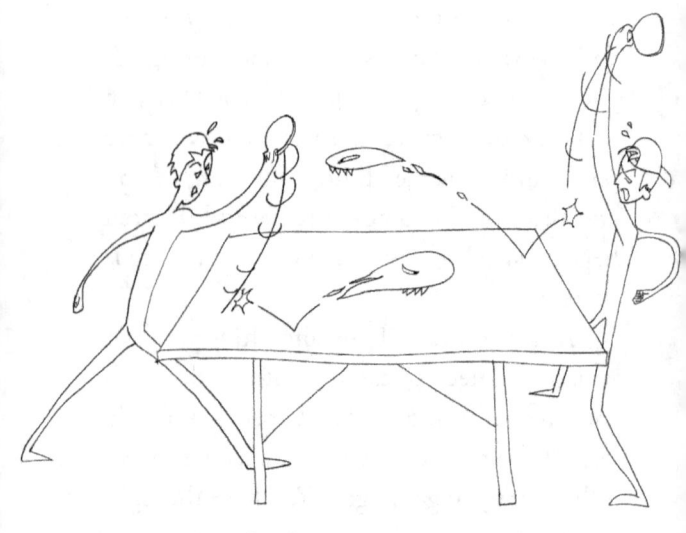

« It is like a ping-pong of negative deeds. »

Then they will not just sit there and do nothing and soon it is like a ping-pong of negative deeds. I say a bad thing; they say a worse thing. I go and kick them; they come and beat me. Me and my people go and kill them, they come and kill more of us and then we cannot forgive. All these long term conflicts can go on for hundreds of years. And hatred can never end hatred. It *has* to end with forgiveness. It has to end with, "Okay, now I stop." If one can see that, then that is forgiveness. This is why you need to do something about anger and hatred as soon as possible, and why you need to work on them directly.

There was once a king in India, called King Ashoka. At first, he was very violent. He killed his brothers and became king and then he conquered most of the country. But when he went to do battle in the south of India, he saw so much death and so much suffering on both sides that he was very upset.

When his army was camping near a river, he saw a man shouting and dancing on the other side. "I won! Now I have got victory!"

And then he threw his sword into the river. King Ashoka asked his people to go and arrest the man, so they brought him to the king. "What do you mean by this?" King Ashoka asked. "You threw your sword in the river and now you say you are the winner. How can you have victory when you have thrown away your sword?"

The man said, "I have a conflict with my neighbour that has been going on for generations. There have been a lot of murders and court cases on both sides. I take revenge and they take revenge. Then I take revenge and they take revenge. But then I saw that it should not be like this. If one side can stop, then the other side will also stop. Otherwise it will go on forever. Now it is my turn to take revenge, but I want to stop this going on. It is difficult for me because of all the pain and sorrow, but I think this is the best way. So I threw my sword into the river and then I felt so relieved. I am the winner because I can forgive and because I am not going to continue with this revenge."

«I won! Now I have got victory!»

King Ashoka was deeply changed by this. He stopped fighting, he declared peace and he became one of the most noble, peaceful and tolerant kings. He did lots of positive things, and he was the main person who spread Buddhism to Sri Lanka and many other countries in Asia.

So that is the idea, to understand deeply that it is not good to hold on to hatred because it only gives pain and problems. If somebody does something wrong, I should try to stop it if I can, but I should not sustain hatred, because that is the worst thing for me and it doesn't help anybody.

Some people think anger is necessary. Without anger, they say, how do you fight against injustice? You need to fight injustice because there is a lot of injustice in the world.

From the Buddhist point of view, you cannot fight injustice with anger. When anger takes over, you lose clarity of mind, and if your rational mind is blurred by anger, then how would you fight injustice? You overreact in the flare of your anger and then you regret it and have to apologize later on. There is a lot of energy when the anger is there, but as soon as it is gone, you are tired, finished, with no energy left. This is not the way to fight injustice. The Buddhist view is that you have to try to fight injustice with compassion.

Two things can happen when you see an injustice is being done. You can focus your mind on the people who do it, or you can focus your mind on the issue. If you focus on the people, then it can become like, "This is very bad. They need to be punished. He needs to be killed." And that doesn't solve the issue, because your anger is targeting the person. Eventually it becomes a personal thing and you just get angry and upset. But if you focus on the issue itself, then it's more like, "This action is not just and should be reversed. Whoever is doing it for whatever reason, it is not right and it should not happen."

When you focus on the action, it becomes compassion because you want to change things for the better. You are not accusing this person, you are not angry and you don't have a personal issue with them. You have an issue-based problem. If the injustice could be reversed, it would be good for the people who have to endure it, and good for the people who do it. So therefore, you are not full of hate. You wish good for everybody, and that is compassion.

The energy that compassion gives is unlike the energy that anger gives. It is sustainable because you want to do something good for everybody. And how do you do that? You think and you act patiently. When you are driven by that kind of motivation, you remain in that compassionate state of mind and you cannot be so overpowered by your emotions that you are unable to think straight. Therefore, from the Buddhist point of view, it is understood that this is the better way of fighting against injustice.

It is actually the only good way. There might have been an injustice, but if you go and do the same to the other people, then that is not justice. It just becomes tit for tat. So, this kind of patience is coming from a deep understanding of what would be good for me and for everybody, now and in the longer term.

If somebody does or says something that makes me angry, that is my habitual tendency. But then I have to think, is it right that I am angry? Is it good for me or not? Usually it is not good for me because anger is a suffering and the more I brood on it the worse it becomes. I don't think anybody says, "Oh, I had such a wonderful morning, I was so angry." You lose sleep because of anger, you lose peace of mind and if you take action influenced by that anger, you always do something that is not good for others. And that has repercussions.

When I am totally overwhelmed by a big anger I can kill somebody, but I can also harm myself. People have been known to kill themselves under the strong influence of anger. It is extremely negative and extremely dangerous. So we try to understand, we try to think carefully. Why am I getting angry? It is because I don't want to be hurt, because I don't want to be unhappy, because I don't want to suffer. Actually, if you look a little more deeply, the anger is making you suffer more. Therefore, the more you can let it go, the better it is for you now, and the better for you later also.

You might say, "If somebody is angry with me, how can I *not* be angry with them?" But if somebody is angry with you, is it really necessary that you get angry also? Maybe you have to see why this person is angry. You know, many times it is not that he is angry with *you*, he is angry because he is in trouble. He is suffering and in pain. Maybe it is because of something you did, but maybe not. It could be a misunderstanding, because if you are nervous and have a lot of tension, then you see everything as dark and bad. Sometimes it is like that. So, when you can see that this person is really angry and upset, you will be sympathetic. "Poor man, he is going through a difficult time. Maybe I should not disturb him for a while. I don't have to say something bad to make it even more hurtful." And many times, if you are kind, people can change.

Sometimes we need patience with our own actions also. For example, if I say, "I will do something destructive if I react with anger now, so let me cool down a bit. Let me delay my reaction." And many times, you know, within ten minutes the anger goes away. It is that temporary, that insubstantial.

Then why can't we give it up? Why can't we stop? There is no reason why we can't stop. We just need a little bit of patience.

We usually think that these emotions are very strong and very kind of solid, but actually they're not that permanent. You need a lot of fuel to keep up a negative emotion like anger. You have to say, "This person did this to me. It is really bad. It is intolerable." And "Yes! Last year also he said something," and then, "The year before also, he said something." You can sometimes go back to either his parents or his community and his country. "Yes! It's because he is English!" So, you have to remember everything and it is not just a little effort, you know. It seems to come naturally, but actually, it is our habit.

« You know, the yak is a very strong animal, but if you put a ring in its nose, then even a child can lead it. »

Some people are influenced by psychology. They think, "Oh I can't touch my emotions. If I suppress them, they will become a problem. I have to be totally led by my emotions as if there is a thread attached to my nose." You know, the yak is a very strong animal, much stronger than a cow, but if you put a ring in its nose, then even a little child can lead it.

I think it is not necessary to give up our freedom to our emotions. I feel that you can let things go so that there is nothing to repress. For instance, if somebody tells me that so-and-so is saying bad things about me I might get angry. Later, I find out that he never actually said that, so what happens to my anger? It is gone, no? There is nothing that I need to suppress or repress or anything like that. It is fully gone because there was no reason to get angry.

Many people used to tell me, "My mother told me not to get angry and now I have a problem because I repressed it." At first I didn't understand how there could be such a powerful mother. I have a lot of respect and love for my mother but she cannot order my emotions around, so what kind of Supermother is this? Then slowly I found out that actually it's not that they didn't get angry. They did get angry, but didn't act it out. That is keeping a grudge, not getting rid of anger. When we say, "Let go," we are not saying to keep it inside, we are saying let it go from the bottom of your heart, from seeing that there is no benefit in getting angry. If you can deeply see that, then you don't have to keep it, so therefore there's nothing to repress. I think this is very important to understand.

Emotions are a little bit like nettles. Now, I really like nettle soup. It is more or less the only vegetable we had in Tibet. It grows wild and when we go for a picnic we make a nice nettle soup and have it with tsampa. Nettles sting if you touch them lightly, but if you grab them firmly, then there's no problem. Emotions are a little bit like that. If you are like, "Oh, I cannot touch my emotions," then they rule over you.

So this kind of patience is about slowly

learning and training not to be overpowered by our anger, hatred and ill will, through seeing very clearly that it is not good for me, or for anybody.

There is another type of impatience that is like intolerance or small mindedness: "I have my own way of thinking, my own way of doing things, and I think that is the only way. My belief is the only truth, so anybody believing or understanding or thinking any other way is totally wrong."

Intolerance and impatience are the source of a lot of conflict, injustice, ignorance and misunderstanding. So, patience here means being able to open my mind, being able to be more spacious and more tolerant.

From the Buddhist point of view, the understanding is that different people need different things. People have different attitudes, different aptitudes, different cultures, different ways of doing things and different interests. When one understands this, then one can become more tolerant and your mind becomes a little bit more spacious and accommodating.

Of course, wisdom is the important element needed for this to really become Paramita, or to become perfection. If patience is accompanied by wisdom, then it becomes the Paramita of Patience. If it is not accompanied by wisdom, then it is patience, but not the Paramita of Patience. Likewise, generosity without wisdom is generosity, but not the Paramita of Generosity. So the wisdom has to be there. We will talk particularly about that wisdom later on.

Generosity and discipline are also the basis for patience. By learning to open your heart and learning how to give and let go, you learn how to be disciplined. And the more you know how to control your actions, how to be flexible and how to act with your body, speech and especially your mind, the more it helps you learn to be patient. This is actually an action. Maybe it is primarily an action of the mind.

«So patience here means being able to open my mind, being able to be more spacious and more tolerant.»

When you understand that negative actions of the mind are useless and that they create lots of pain for yourself and others, you see that you should not hold onto them. Since you have learnt to let go and you have trained in discipline, you can see that there is no need to be angry and that it is more necessary to be kind and compassionate.

From the Buddhist point of view, you can be compassionate to even the most negative people, who have done the worst things. Of course you don't admire them. Never. You know how horrible they were and what bad things they did. But if you believe in the consequences of karma, you know that if somebody does something really negative, the one who is most harmed is themselves. You know that people who do negative things out of ignorance, misguidedness and negative emotions, do so much harm to others and especially so much harm to themselves. So, when you see that you don't need to hate them. You feel sorry for them. You feel pity for them. Of course, if you can, you should stop them.

I would like to relate a question that somebody asked the 17th Karmapa. They asked, "If somebody slaps you on the right cheek, should you turn your left cheek or not, because Jesus Christ said you should?" I liked Karmapa's answer very much. He said, if you turn your left cheek, what you are doing is thinking about your own karma. If he slaps you on the right cheek and you give your left cheek, then you are safe, you have done very nicely, but you are not thinking about the karma of the person who is slapping you. He is doing a very bad thing, you know. So, if you are concerned about the karma of that person, you might stop him, if you can. Not out of hatred, or anger, but out of compassion. I think that is the understanding. If this person does something very bad to me or other people, it is also not good for him. So, if I can see that, then why not stop him from doing it?

There is a Jataka story of the Bodhisattva actually killing someone with this kind of intention. Once, the Buddha was born as a sailor working on a ship that was carrying hundreds of people across the ocean. Somehow, this sailor found out that a man was planning to kill the captain and hijack the ship. He was going to murder everybody and take everything for himself. The sailor was a very compassionate, courageous man. He thought, "I can't let this happen. Maybe I will go to a hell realm. Maybe for many lifetimes I will be killed by something, but for the sake of this man and to save all the other people on this ship, I have to go through the negative karma of killing him." So he killed the man, and saved all the people.

This action of killing was not without negative effect and it is said that the sailor died violently for many lifetimes. But actually, from a Buddhist point of view, through that action he also came many kalpas nearer to enlightenment. I think Buddha told this story when something happened and he got hurt and then he said, "This is the last time this will happen."

This is not to say that you have to do these bad things. Especially as there is always this danger that we are just finding an excuse because we have a very clever ego. "You know, I did it because it is for the good of everybody."

This is the understanding.

Questioner: If you are around somebody who has a tendency to be angry and you can see that it's harming them, as well as other people and yourself, is it a good idea to actually point it out? Or should you just keep it to yourself and kind of let them get on with it?

Rinpoche: You can try. Why not? Sometimes you can get into the habit of debating and if somebody says something, I have to say something against it. It can become a little nasty after a while. A colleague of mine was very short tempered. When anything happened she would get angry and then she would get into trouble. I used to tell her, "Don't be like that, why are you doing this?" and she said, "It just happens." She asked me to remind her, so when she was about to lose her temper at staff meetings or things like that, I'd tap her and then she would look. After some years, she really changed completely and I didn't have to tap her. She'd look at me and laugh. She was not a negative, grudging kind of person, just short tempered, so some kind of reminder like that actually seemed to help.

Questioner: Rinpoche, I'm wondering whether our culture of therapy is actually feeding the fire of our emotions, rather than helping us move into a more positive way of relating to them?

Rinpoche: I don't know much about therapies and psychology and things like that, but I feel that many of these therapies are done for people who don't have a very strong ego. First we need a good healthy samsaric ego with lots of anger, desire and pride. Then, when we become a healthy, samsaric being we try to work on that and to transcend samsara. I think the therapies are helping to make robust, samsaric people, but I don't think they are necessarily geared to transcend samsara. That is another matter.

Questioner: I'm curious about this idea that you had about somebody holding onto anger? I'm curious to know how that could even happen. What is the process with something that hasn't really got any substance?

Rinpoche: I think we can keep a grudge or a hurt feeling for a very long time. We have a habit of remembering and holding onto bad things and then forgetting the good things. Say you have a friend, or say your parents have done so many good things and then one time they are upset or angry and say something bad, or do something unkind. So, forgetting all those good things, you hold on to that one bad thing all your life. Sometimes I have seen that.

Questioner: I work with children. I can understand that process in someone with more history, but with a child, how can that happen?

Rinpoche: We have lots of traumas, which we keep in a kind of unconscious or subconscious state of mind. This gives us a lot of fear, but we sometimes don't know why we feel that way. From the Buddhist point of view, these traumas are coming from the experience of death and birth, as well as from previous lives. But from the psychological point of view, it has to be from this life. Therefore, it could be from childhood, or from some time like that. That is what they say.

I think it is true that some children can have many traumas. I know one person who was tortured by her father and she has a lot of resentment because of that. Once, I really tried to go into this more deeply and asked what exactly he did and she said, "Well, he used to put me on a chair and he used to play the piano for hours." I said, "The poor father. Maybe he was trying to entertain you. Maybe he was just not a good musician." But she didn't like that. She felt bad because she had to sit there for a long time. I think maybe he didn't allow her to move too much.

Sometimes, it is in your mind. You don't know the source of your bad feeling. It's how you take it, no? I think it is not necessarily something really cruel.

Questioner: I'm really glad that you brought up the idea of children being taught that they're naughty if they're angry, because that happened to me. When I was angry my mother told me I shouldn't be angry and there was a punishment. So I learned that if I was angry I was not an alright person and I've had to struggle with that as an adult. When I got into relationships, the anger I was experiencing leaked out in ways that I could pretend were nothing to do with me. I think that's true of a lot of people, particularly in this country where we're all very buttoned up, you know. It's not alright to be emotional, shall we say. I think it's very easy then to say, "Oh, I just don't get angry," and you sort of leapfrog over it. What I'm trying to say is, you can't let go of anger until you actually know you've got it.

Rinpoche: That is very true. I think that's very important. We have to acknowledge the problem before we can do something about it. And we do deny lots of things, you know. We don't want to talk about bad things, even death. We know that we are afraid of death, but we can't say anything about it, "Are you afraid of death?" "No, I'm not afraid." But actually we are afraid of death. Once, I was giving a talk and people were asked "Are you afraid of death?" Only ten or fifteen people said yes. "Are you afraid of getting fat?" Everybody said yes. I'm sure they are not more afraid of becoming fat than of death, but you know, there are many things we deny. We react but we deny it and then we hold onto it.

Questioner: What I got from your talk, Rinpoche, was how strong compassion can be. Sometimes I think compassion is soft and internal and inactive, but for the first time I really got what you were saying about how you meet anger with compassion. So, I suppose I'm asking you about that moment of transformation from anger into compassion?

Rinpoche: Many people think that compassion is soft and kind of passive. It doesn't need to be. Compassion can be as strong and as forceful as anger. I think this is very important to understand. It actually only requires a different way of looking at things, because when you are angry you say, "I am hurt, I am angry." But if you become more clear about the person who is instrumental in making you angry, you will find that they are not totally doing it just to hurt you, or that they are not free of other pressures. And when you see this very clearly, you see that it is not necessary to be so angry, because in a way, that person is also being used as an instrument. There are many forces and many things going on. Therefore it is not just about that person, it is about everything else, and this person is as much a victim as I am. So when you see this big picture, then I think you can see it in a different way. Sometimes, the reasoning is given like this:

"If somebody hits you on your head with a stick, why are you angry?"

"Because he hit me with a stick and I have a pain in my head."

"Then why are you not angry with the stick, because the stick is the one that hit you?"

"No, you can't say a stick is responsible because it can't just come and hit me. It is lifted by the hand and then it hits me."

"Then why don't you hate the hand?"

"The hand is just an instrument. This person uses his hand to lift the stick, so actually this person is the one who did it."

"Then is it this person? If he is not angry will he hit you?

"No, if he is not angry, he is not hitting."

"Then it is actually anger that makes this person use his hand to pick up this stick and hit your head? So why don't you get angry with the anger?"

If you look a little bit more clearly, it is possible to see that there is not one thing that you hate and one thing that is angry, it is a consequence of many causes and conditions. Therefore, this person is also more or less a victim. When you can see this a little bit deeply, I think it changes your perspective.

Questioner: Rinpoche, I find that it's very comfortable once you've let go of a big anger. However, there are other situations where you might think you have an analytical mind about something, but actually you are still holding on to a subtle level of anger. How can we see that we are really letting go and not in denial about letting go?

Rinpoche: I think we have to train step by step. We cannot say that we have no anger at all, but a little bit better is a little bit better, so I think we have to see it like this. I think the exercise is to try to do it every day. I try to forgive. Sometimes we do what we call Vajrasattva practice. This is a practice of purification through an exercise of the mind. I want to let go of negative emotions and negative things that I have done and that have happened to me, those I remember and those I don't remember. In this practice, I feel that a nectar, or purifying substance, comes through my body and I feel totally purified so that I don't keep the negativity in my body, or in any of my cells. I feel as if I have let it all go, completely. I feel myself to be crystal clear, transparent, shining like a rainbow. And then I let go of everything and try to feel only kindness and compassion. The training is to do this again and again.

Sometimes you have something specific to work on, like feelings of hurt or anger, but sometimes you don't have anything like that. You don't have to think of a specific thing, but in general, anything that you hold onto, anything like negative emotions and hurt feelings, you let go and let go and let go. That is the practice.

Questioner: Rinpoche, I just wanted to share some advice that you gave me a while ago. I came to you saying what do I do with all this hurt and you pointed out that the perpetrator is long gone, but each time I think about it I relive it and the only person I'm hurting is myself. Somehow, that really helped me. And I would say that you know when you are beginning to let go when it begins to stop hurting.

Questioner: Rinpoche, the Five Buddha Families promise to help us with overcoming certain negativities, like Buddha Akshobhya overcoming anger. How do we practice that?

Rinpoche: Yes, if we can understand the nature of emptiness, or the true nature of ourselves and of all phenomena, then there is nothing that has anger, either from anybody or towards anybody. That is the wisdom part of it. Buddha Akshobhya, what we call the clear light, or mirror-like wisdom, is basically understanding the nature of anger, or the nature of emotions. Generally, anger comes and goes, appears and disappears. It becomes a negative emotion because you are confused. You think there is somebody to be hurt, somebody who will hurt you and something called hurt. You kind of designate, "I am. I am hurt," and all these designations are actually made by the mind. But if you look deeply, you see that there is nothing that is called hurt. What is it that is hurt? What "is," are interdependent entities with no true substance.

Because our feeling of hurt or anger is restricting our wisdom, we have difficulty in experiencing this brilliance, this wisdom shining like solar energy, and we make it into "This is me, this is others. Others do this, it's not good for me" and then we get hurt, we get angry, we get upset. The clearer I become, the more unobstructed and unobscured I am, the more I see that there is nothing called anger. What we call anger is actually nothing but compassion because there is nothing to hold onto. Anger comes because you are holding on to something. That is the essence of Akshobhya, or Vajrasattva, or mirror-like wisdom.

4
THE PARAMITA OF
Diligence

The fourth Paramita is the Paramita of Diligence. As we discussed, all these Paramitas are actually about working on our habitual tendencies and working on transforming ourselves. Step by step, we are training ourselves in how to react in a less negative way and slowly learning how to react in a more positive way.

I think it is very important to understand that from the Buddhist point of view, there is nothing that is ultimately bad, or ultimately good. The right thing is in contrast to something else. Something you do can be worse than something else, or something you do can be better than something else. It is always relative. Then, depending on your situation and on the circumstances, you work to try and make it more positive and less negative. That is the whole point.

So therefore, when you take the bodhisattva vow, you say: "Just as the buddhas of the past generated the bodhisattva's attitude, and trained on the path step by step, so I too would like to generate bodhicitta for the benefit of everybody."

Diligence is basically understood as a joy in doing positive things. It is said to be very important because it is seen as the support for every good thing and for how to train. It is not about pushing yourself too hard, but generating and developing a joyful way of doing something positive. If we just push hard and there is no joy in doing it, we will feel aversion, and once we feel it as a burden, then sooner or later we will stop doing it. The longer we carry a burden, the heavier it becomes. And when it becomes too difficult we have to throw it off. So there is always an insistence that diligence should have the joy of doing things, in order to inspire ourselves and to feel happy in doing something.

We have no problem doing negative things, but we don't like to do positive things. That is our usual habit. People sometimes have a lot of energy for doing things that are not so good, but I don't think that's necessarily bad. I was in Ibiza recently and there were lots of people in the airport. It seems that many of them come without booking a hotel. They go to dance clubs the whole night and then go to the beach all day, so they don't need hotels!

Now, why are we not happy doing positive things? From the Buddhist point of view, we call it laziness. In order to understand diligence, we first have to work on our laziness.

I am an expert on laziness. I call myself Lazy Lama, but not because I am not doing anything. I think you can see how much I am traveling. What I am lazy at is my practice. I have received lots of teachings, I have had lots of good teachers and I know how to practise Dharma, more or less. I know how useful and how beneficial it would be for me to practise Dharma. So why am I not practising? Laziness!

There was once a monk in Dzogchen monastery, very near to where my mother comes from. This monk had a friend who was a spirit, so he was very comfortable because this spirit would bring him whatever he wanted.

The monk said, "You are a spirit, so you know more or less when people die."

"Yes, I can see that," said the spirit.

"Remind me when I'm nearing death," the monk said, "so that I really practise dharma."

The spirit said, "Definitely I'll remind you."

So, the monk just enjoyed his life, and then one day the spirit came and said excitedly, "There is white hair on your head."

"I've had white hair for some time now. Why are you so excited about that?"

"You knew that?"

"Of course I knew."

The spirit said, "Oh, I see," and he went away.

Then another day the spirit came and said, "Look! Your teeth! Some of your teeth are gone."

"That's nothing new," the monk said. "My teeth have been slowly going for a while."

"Oh, you knew it."

"Of course I knew. They're *my* teeth."

"Okay then. No problem." And the spirit went away again.

Then one day the spirit appeared and said, "I think you are going to die tomorrow."

"What?!!"

«The spirit came and said excitedly, «There is white hair on your head.»»

"You are going to die tomorrow."

The monk said, "But I *told* you to remind me a long time before."

"Of course I reminded you."

"You never said anything. I don't remember you reminding me about dying."

"Well, I said your hair is becoming white and you knew about it," said the spirit. "I said your teeth are falling out and you knew about it. So I thought you knew about it."

Basically, we talk about three types of laziness. One is not doing what you want to do, or what you need to do. Delaying. Putting off. Hasta manana. Procrastination is a word I was very proud to learn. When I learnt English, I actually had very few classes. As our teacher was the Director of the Institute, he didn't have much time, so all he taught was eighty-six verbs. The rest I just studied from the dictionary. I knew lots of words and how to spell them, but I didn't know how to pronounce them. So when I learnt a big, long word I felt very proud. PRO-CRAST-IN-ATION. So nice. I wanted to be very diligent, so I wrote down

EL-IM-IN-ATE PRO-CRAST-IN-ATION and hung it in my room. I felt so knowledgeable. Then one of my friends came when I was not there. He waited a little bit, then he saw ELIMINATE PROCRASTINATION and he wrote below it: FROM TOMORROW. So that became my motto. Eliminate Procrastination From Tomorrow.

This is usually what we call laziness. We know what to do, we know it should be done, we know it is good to do it, but we don't do it and then we feel bad for not doing it. Yet somehow, we still don't do it.

This is because of many different reasons. Sometimes we like to rest, or we want to be distracted. Sometimes, we just say, "I'm tired," or we have something else to do. It's as if in some way our enthusiasm, or our inspiration is not so strong, so we want to enjoy ourselves and do something else.

ELIMINATE PROCRASTINATION

What we need to do is to see that a little bit of urgency is important. We try to inspire ourselves by thinking about impermanence, and about the positive effect of doing those things. We try to see how important, and how necessary it is to get these things accomplished. If we are not inspired, then we will not do them. So, seeing the benefits of doing positive things and the faults of not doing those things generates this kind of diligence.

Diligence is not only about the intensity of doing something, but about the regularity of doing it also. If you really want to get something accomplished, then you have to do it consistently. Not running, running, but consistently and slowly. If I want to go to a faraway place and I just get up and start running, maybe I can run ten or twenty kilometers, but after that I'm so exhausted that I cannot run any more and I may not be even be able to walk the next day, so I cannot reach the faraway place. I need to prepare myself if I have to go somewhere. Maybe I need to get a good pair of shoes, maybe I need to have some provisions and walking sticks and things like that. And then, I walk slowly.

Sometimes people from Tibet prostrate from Kham to Lhasa, from Lhasa to Kathmandu and from Kathmandu to Bodhgaya. I have seen people who have done that, and it is not easy, you know. I saw one person doing that from Kathmandu to Bodhgaya and the first day he just did three rounds of the Boudha Stupa. The second day, just one kilometer down from Boudha Stupa, and then he kind of progressed slowly, slowly. I was there when he arrived in Bodhgaya. It was quite amazing. We were all sitting around the Bodhgaya Temple. Everybody had colds and coughs and wore face masks and then this person came along the dusty road doing prostrations, going *shhwisshh, shhwisshh*, like this. He made three rounds of the outer ring and then he came down the stairs *shhwisshh, shhwisshh*. Then he went to see the Karmapa with a scarf and there he stopped. And next day he shaved and he was *glowing*. No cold, no cough. Not even that much thinner. He didn't look like he had come all this way, just totally fresh. Amazing.

The understanding is that when you have this kind of determination and strong kind of inspiration and you persevere, then little by little, you can go very far and do many things. Those who go slowly get there faster, they say.

The second laziness is that you are very busy doing lots of things but you don't do anything useful and important. Many people are like, "Oh, this is kind of interesting, I'll do it. Oh, *this* is also interesting! Oh, *this* is also interesting and enjoyable!" So you do this and that and you run here and there, and then at the end of the day, or the end of your life you say, "What have I actually done?" You don't have anything concrete, anything that has really benefited other people, or really transformed yourself. Then you know that you have been lazy. People sometimes call it the laziness of busyness. Because you are very busy, you have too many things to do and you have no time, but what do you really achieve?

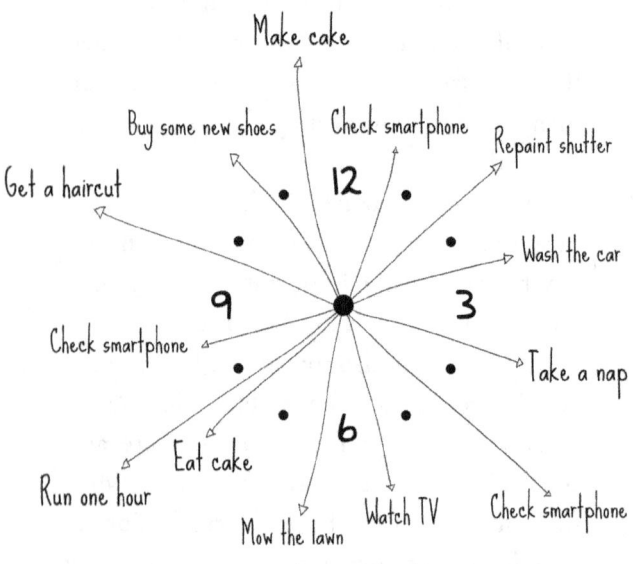

« The second laziness is that you are very busy doing lots of things but you don't do anything that is really useful and important. »

What this shows is that we need to learn how to have the right priorities. What is the most important thing? Of course, every one of us has only twenty-four hours a day, and then we need to sleep. Then sometimes it is also possible that *not* doing something might be more useful. If it is something bad or something harmful, then not doing it is better. We cannot do everything that we feel like doing. We must limit ourselves to what is most appropriate, useful and beneficial at this time. So, learning to prioritize is important. Sometimes, you choose something because it is interesting, and then you feel, "Actually, if I look more deeply, doing something else would be much more useful for me and for other people, but I am kind of attached to this thing." Letting go of certain habits, or certain things which take a lot of time and energy and do not really benefit too much, is not easy. Therefore, learning to essentialize the important things is also an aspect of diligence.

It is not that you cannot rest. Sometimes, taking time off is important. You have a break for a few days, or maybe a few months, with the intention that you get relaxed and rejuvenated before you come back. Rejuvenating your energy is part of diligence.

The third laziness is what they call *da nyi nyepa*, or "insulting yourself" laziness. Many of us have this kind of thing. "I can't do it. I will not be able to do it." You don't have self-confidence. Even before you try, you decide you are too small, too bad, too unintelligent. This is regarded as the worst kind of laziness because if you decide that you will not be able to do something, then you will never do it and so you never achieve it, because you already decided without even trying, that it is not possible for you. You belittle yourself too much. You don't appreciate your potential or want to explore it. You don't even want to try. From the Buddhist point of view, everybody has the potential to become enlightened, so everybody has the potential to accomplish anything. Some people can do it more easily, some people have to train more. But, why not? That's the idea.

So, it is not about whether I can do it or not, it is about whether it should be done or not. That is why we talked about the bodhisattva's attitude in the beginning: "I see a lot of suffering in this world. I see lots of people with lots of problems. All this pain must stop. Everybody should be happy and joyful, and have lasting peace and I am going to work towards that. It doesn't matter how long it may take, or how hard it may be. It doesn't matter if anybody helps me or not, I have to do this. Maybe I am not strong enough now. Maybe I don't have great abilities, but I will train and sooner or later I will get it done." That is how a bodhisattva trains. It is said that if you start doing it, however small and powerless you are, if you do it, even the King of the Gods will come and help you.

There is a Jataka Story about diligence and courage. It is said that once the Buddha was a small parrot living in a forest. One day there was a big forest fire. The parrot was flying away when she heard the anguished cries of all the animals and insects who were surrounded by the fire. The little parrot was very moved by their suffering. She thought, "How can I just go away and do nothing? I must do something to help these people."

So she flew to the river and dipped into the water and then came back and fluttered her wings over the forest fire. She went back and did this again and again and again. The fire was very hot. She was choking with the smoke and all her feathers were singed, but still she kept going.

Up in heaven, the young gods were looking down and laughing. "Look at this foolish parrot. What does she think she is doing?"

"This little parrot thinks that she is going to put out this big forest fire by little sprinkles of her feathers. Some people can be so foolish."

«Big bird, you don't need to tell me what to do or what not to do. You are so big! Come and help me.»

Diligence

«The King of the Gods was so moved by the courage and the determination of this small, little parrot that he started to shed tears.»

At that moment, Indra, the King of the Gods, was passing and his attention was caught by what the young gods were saying. He wanted to test what was happening, so he turned into a big eagle and appeared just above this little parrot. "Little parrot! What do you think you are doing? Do you think you can put out this big fire with your little sprinkle of water? You better save your life while you can."

And the parrot looked up and said, "You don't need to tell me what to do or what not to do, big bird. Come and help me! You are so big and we need to put this fire out now."

So, the King of the Gods, who was also the God of Rain, was so moved by the courage and determination of this tiny little parrot that he started to shed tears. And because he was the Rain God, his tears fell as lots of rain and the forest fire was put out.

Some of his tears fell on the parrot because she was just under him. Suddenly, the burned and singed feathers grew again. With each teardrop, a different colored feather grew.

So, the little parrot succeeded in extinguishing the forest fire and she also got new feathers. That is why parrots have these very colourful feathers. It is a nice story, no?

I think this kind of determination and ambition is important because sometimes in Buddhism, when we talk about trying to reduce aversion or attachment, people think, "Oh, you just want to become like nothing. You don't want to do anything. The highest thing is no ambition, no attraction, no emotion, no nothing."

That is not the idea. Not loving and not having attachment are two different things. Attachment is about me. Loving is about the other. It is not to say that you should not have any ambition. One should have *great* ambitions, not small ambitions, or wrong ambitions that can lead to problems for oneself and others. Or maybe you don't know what you want.

So, ambition should be there; the greater the better. Because if you have very high and great ambitions, then you will work towards that aim, and if you work for the greatest benefit, then other things come your way. If your ambition is only for a small thing, then you will never achieve that great ambition. And if you have a wrong ambition, you know, it doesn't really do much good.

Once, a man got a wish-fulfilling boon. "You can wish for anything. One wish and it will be granted." The man said, "I wish my wife was twenty years younger than me," and then he became twenty years older! So, if you don't do it properly, whatever you wish for might not be so good. There are many stories which show this.

So, slowly and patiently, working consistently step by step, diligence overcomes these three different kinds of laziness with enthusiasm and inspiration, and without getting discouraged.

One thing is to clarify your goal, or your destination. Another is to inspire yourself, make friends with what you do and do it lightly, not turning it into a burden. We can view something we do as very interesting and very joyful, or we can see the same thing as heavy and very difficult. It really depends on our way of seeing it.

Sometimes, especially in the West, I have found that hobbies are sometimes a very hard job. I used to see pictures of the sea with all the sailboats and the masts, and people lying down on the deck. So I thought, "Oh, fantastic, so nice." And then I was invited to go on this kind of sailing boat and I was very excited. "Yes! We must go!" Oh, it is so much hard work, with everybody running around. Also, a little bit dangerous, you know. The boom almost broke my head.

There was a man I knew, who liked to climb mountains. He fell and broke his back and for several years he couldn't walk properly. Then one day, I got an email from him. He has a wife and children and he writes, "I'm going mountain climbing in Russia. If I die, please pray for me." What is this, you know? Why do you have to risk your life? He is not inexperienced. He knows he could die. So these hobbies can be very hard work, can be very dangerous and expensive and yet people have no problem doing them. I haven't seen anybody saying, "Oh, my hobby is such hard work!"

Well then, what is supposed to be work? In India, people sometimes carry a *hundred kilos* on their back and then they walk uphill sweating all day long. But here? You just drive a very comfortable car on a very nice road. The car is heated or cooled, and then you park and go to the office in a very nice, clean, beautiful, carpeted room. You sit on a chair at your own desk and then what do you do? Maybe type a letter or make a telephone call. No carrying a hundred kilos. Have a little chat and a nice cup of coffee or tea and then, "I'm so tired." The hobby could be work, and work could be a hobby, you know. Why? Just because of the way you see it, no? If I say this is work, then this is work.

«The hobby could be work, and work could be hobby...»

When I was working in the university, lots of students used to come and ask for advice. "I want an interesting profession. What should I do?" So, I thought, if you want to do something interesting, maybe take up sports? But as soon as it became work, sport was not that interesting anymore. You cannot really find work that always remains interesting. Also, we change and something that seems interesting now may become less interesting after a time. So then I started to say, "Maybe you should look for something that might be useful to society, because even if it is not so interesting, at least you feel that there is a purpose if you can see that it is doing good." Many people have no job satisfaction and the real cause is not the pay, you know. The pay could be quite high and still there is no job satisfaction. I found that the main cause is when they find that what they do is not helping anybody. When we see in a clear way that what we do is really beneficial for lots of people, I think that can make us more joyful and enthusiastic.

They say that three things are necessary to really practice dharma: diligence, devotion and wisdom. Devotion is to understand what we are doing clearly. Diligence is that you want to do it and you are doing it in an enthusiastic way. And wisdom is your understanding, knowing how things really are. So, when these three things are there you accomplish a lot.

Sometimes we need to remind ourselves to make friends with meditation, or to make the Six Paramitas like a hobby, because if you are interested, then it becomes a hobby. So diligence is something like that.

Questioner: I was so interested in the analogy of the nettles. There is a phrase, "grasping the nettle" and I think it's very true. I just wondered though, it is quite a big step to go from being very tentative, to really full-on grasping the nettle and confronting the difficulty. Would you say something about that?

Rinpoche: If we act and react under the influence of a negative emotion, then we create lots of problems for ourselves, and lots of pain for other people around us. We think that this emotion is too powerful and we cannot do anything about it because, "it's my emotion." I think that is wrong, because what I do and what I want to do has to be under my power. If I do and say everything that comes into my mind, I will be considered mad, no? It is normal that different thoughts come, but we don't follow everything that comes up. We should have some kind of discrimination.

So, if anger comes up, or too much attachment, or jealousy or whatever, then you have to say, "Should I or should I not follow this?" And if you can clearly see that following this will get you into trouble, you say, "I don't need to go that way, I don't need to act this out." When you know this, then you can let go. That doesn't mean that it might not come back again, but that is okay. You can again ask yourself and clearly see and then let go. I think you will be much happier afterwards. For example, if I had thoughts about doing something that wasn't right and then I didn't do it, I would feel better afterwards because I had made the right decision. And the decision doesn't harm me, or give me trauma, or repress anything. You just say to yourself, "This is the way it should be." So I don't need to fear that I have to do everything that my emotions dictate.

Questioner: Rinpoche, your story about being hit with a stick and asking, "What am I angry with, am I angry with the hand, or the person?" made me think that actually, I'm not angry, I'm afraid of being hit again. It's the same thing with laziness- a fear of being overwhelmed, or a fear of failure. With the story of the stick, it's easier to see the anger as useless and to let go of it, but fear is a different thing. There seems to be no stick, no person to identify and no hand hitting you. I wondered if you have any advice on that?

Rinpoche: Yes, fear is said to be the root of all negative emotions. Anger, attachment, greed and jealousy all come from fear. Even arrogance and pride come from fear. You have a fear of being hurt, you fear something bad happening and then it turns into anger and hatred and so on. Sometimes it is said that as long as you have ignorance and confusion, you have a certain level of fear. Therefore, fear is very basic. It is not easy to completely free yourself from fear because it is very deep in us, but we have to work on it. We have all kinds of negative emotions based on fear, but then we also have denial. We need to understand and acknowledge that we have fear and that we can experience fear. I think it is very important to understand that fear does not help. It is a totally useless emotion.

We fear that something might happen, that we might get hit again or whatever. Then the more we fear the stronger it becomes until it becomes panic and we then we start to tremble and get hysterical. People can die of fear. I have examples of two people. One almost died and one actually died. I know a pilot who became a nun. Once she was flying to somewhere in Africa for a conference. There was a man sitting next to her who was sweating and very frightened, because he had been involved in a plane crash once before. So she held his hand and talked to him until they landed. Then, on the return journey, there was an announcement. "Is there a doctor? Somebody is having a health issue." Then the plane landed somewhere it shouldn't have landed and she realised that it was because of this man. He had been so frightened and his blood sugar levels went so far down that the doctors said he would have died if the plane had delayed landing.

Another story is that in Tibet, there was a place that was supposed to be haunted. They said that if you go at night and hammer a peg inside this place and then come back, that you would be rewarded. One person said, "I'm going." So he went there, but he didn't come back and next day, they found him dead. He had hammered the peg through his clothes and then when he was trying to go, he couldn't. He was so frightened thinking that the ghost had got him that he actually died of fear.

However much you fear, it does not prevent what you fear from coming. If it has to come, it will come. Therefore, fear is useless. It doesn't work. Also, fearing is not nice, it is a painful thing. There is a saying, "A coward dies a hundred deaths every day, but a brave man dies only once." If you don't fear, you die. If you fear, you also die. When you have to die you will die, but if you are too afraid of death, then it is like you are dying every day. Every day fear, fear, fear.

«He was so frightened thinking that the ghost had got him…»

If you are afraid, you don't dare to do anything, but if you have less fear you can do things. It is not true that those who fear get fewer problems, and those who do not fear get more. When you get what you fear, or when you die, you get it anyway. So, if you deeply remind yourself of this, I think you can lessen your fear.

My first ever flight was in '87 or '88. Myself and another person were flying from Delhi to Bagdogra. The flight was early morning so we were coming down from our rooms at four o'clock to catch the taxi, and there was someone coming upstairs with an empty glass. My friend, who was a little bit superstitious, said, "Oh! That's really bad. Wherever I go anywhere, if I see something empty, something terrible happens. So maybe we shouldn't fly today, because if something happens in the air there is no chance. And it is a machine, you know." At that time in Sikkim, we had only old cars. Whenever we drove anywhere something always went wrong, so we thought the plane was a little bit like that. But to get another ticket was very difficult, so

I said, "Maybe it's nothing, maybe we should go to the airport."

So we went to the airport and the flight was delayed by four hours. Then the plane took off with lots of rattling and after some time, I felt a lot of pain in my arms. Then I saw that I was holding the seat in front of me, trying to lift the plane up. "Maybe if I could fly this might help" I thought, "but I can't fly, so if the plane crashes, I don't think it would be useful. If I have to die on this flight, then I'll die. I could die in my bed, even if I'm not flying." So I went to sleep.

Since then, whenever I go onto a plane I go to sleep. Sometimes I don't even know when it takes off. I sleep throughout the flight, but I never miss any meals. So that's good because I get to eat everything, drink everything and get lots of sleep. I actually rest more in planes and cars when I'm traveling, than in a bedroom. I can sleep like this, completely, deeply, for many hours, no problem. I don't even get jet lag. Anyway, that's not the point here.

Questioner: Some people try to confront their fears, but you get the odd crazy person that seems to feed on fear and becomes a kind of adrenalin junkie. They feel really strong and they've got all this energy from the adrenalin, so they're super aware of everything around them. That climber friend you spoke about had the responsibility of a wife and a family and yet he was still going back into this thirst for adrenalin. I wondered if you were tempted to say something like, "You asked for prayers, but really what I want you to do is think about the preciousness of human life with every step you take up that mountain." I wonder if you ever think it's not worth trying with somebody, or do you always try?

Rinpoche: He is generally a very responsible person, but he has to climb and so I thought it was not helpful to pressure him. He would feel bad that he didn't listen to me, so I thought it was not useful and didn't say anything. Sometimes people have hesitations and then you can say something. But some people are just like, "This is the way I am" and it doesn't matter what you say, it doesn't work. I said I would pray for him. Maybe I said be careful, life is precious or something, but I don't think I tried to dissuade him from going.

Questioner: Rinpoche, a lot of us here were very fond of Lama Tsering Paljor and I wondered if you'd say a little about him, how fantastic his training was, like his prostrations and his meditation and how, when he was given the bad news about his illness, he took it like going on a picnic. I saw a photo of him about one week before he died, with Lama Soga in hospital, and his eyes were bright. I just wondered if you'd tell us a little bit about him and his training.

Rinpoche: Lama Tsering Paljor was from the Eastern part of Tibet, from the same kind of area I come from. He did a three year retreat in a Nyingma monastery there. He was discipline master and also held lots of responsible posts. He came to Lhasa by prostration. Many people do that in Tibet, although it's very, very hard, because it is extremely cold, with very high altitudes. Walking to Lhasa takes something like three months, so I don't know how long he took, maybe one year, maybe more. Then he came to India and did many three year retreats.

Cancer was diagnosed very late, but he had had this problem for a very long time. Somebody recommended him so I invited him and he stayed in my retreat for quite a few years. He was very nice, very well-mannered and was a very good practitioner. He did lots of *chöd* practice and was very good with his hands. He was very kind and although he didn't speak the language, he could communicate with everybody who came there. I think he was a good teacher. Then he got this cancer of the oesophagus and later he underwent some kind of operations in Kolkata. But it was very difficult. It is a very bad kind of cancer. He wanted to go back to Tibet and die there, and he did succeed in going back. I think he lived about one year, or maybe a little more, and then he passed away. He was a very good practitioner and he had not much fear of death.

5
THE PARAMITA OF
Meditation

The fifth Paramita is the Paramita of Meditation.

Meditation is placed as the fifth paramita because all the other paramitas are a kind of preparation, or good grounding for meditation. All Six Paramitas are interrelated, so you can't exactly say that this is first, this is second and this is third. However, there is a kind of logic about why they are placed in this order. It is because the more we can let things go, the more we become disciplined, the more patient we become, the more we can do positive things joyfully, the more meditation becomes easier and more established.

Meditation has a few different words in Tibetan. One of them is *samten*, which is the translation of Sanskrit word *dhyana*, or in Pali, *jnana*. *Sam* is "mind" and *ten* means "stable", so the training is to make our minds stable, peaceful and very clear. Unshakeable, so that we are not disturbed by all the different things happening around us.

Another word for meditation is gom, which means "getting habituated to" or "becoming acquainted with." It means that whatever state of mind we think is good to become, we do it again and again, and then become habituated to that. We have certain wrong habits in the way we see, the way we feel and the way we act and when we understand that we should not react like that, we try to find out what is the right way and then we use that again and again, so that our habits change.

At the moment, our mind is wild and out of control. If we say, "Now concentrate!" it won't concentrate, and if we say, "Don't think!" it thinks even more.

So how do we stabilise the mind? We can't do it by force. We can't say, "Don't think, don't think, don't think." It doesn't work like that. We need to use a technique and a training. That technique is meditation, and when we know how to do this, it becomes easier to train our mind in the Paramitas and in all other things.

Once, the Bodhisattva was born as a poor farmhand who worked for a very spiritual man. As the entire household was very religious, he was able to practice a little meditation with everyone. Then, because of the good karma arising from his meditation, when this lowly farmhand died, he was reborn as the wise and noble King Udaya.

One day, King Udaya sees a poor beggar singing in the market place outside the palace. He is curious to know the secret of this man's happiness, so he goes down to speak with him. The poor beggar reveals that he has a great treasure hidden at home, so King Udaya decides to test him out. But no matter how much money he offers, the man insists on holding onto his treasure, which is really only a halfpenny hidden behind a loose brick in a wall.

King Udaya is so impressed by the integrity and resolve of the poor beggar, that he names him King Half-penny and invites him to rule half his kingdom.

For a while all is well, but then King Half-penny begins to want the entire kingdom for himself. He becomes so obsessed and broods so much on this idea, that one day he actually finds himself standing next to the sleeping King Udaya with a big sword in his hand, ready to strike. Just in time, he comes to his senses. He wakes his friend and confesses everything.

King Udaya says, "You want the whole kingdom, dear friend? Here, take it." But King Half-penny is so shocked by the way his own endless desires have led him to the brink of committing murder that he decides to leave at once. He goes to the Himalayas to meditate, and after a while, he becomes completely realised.

Back in the palace, King Udaya is being shampooed by his barber, Gangamala. The king is so joyful that he can't help composing a song. Gangamala is fascinated and asks what it means, so Udaya tells him that the song is about how just a small amount of meditation caused him to be reborn as a king, and how that led to King Half-penny renouncing all desire and achieving true freedom.

Gangamala's mind is blown wide open. "This is real freedom," he thinks, "and it is possible even for someone like me." So he throws down his razor and shaving soaps and immediately sets off for the Himalayas.

«Meditate diligently and gain freedom for yourselves.»

A few years later, King Udaya and his courtiers are in the palace gardens when Gangamala flies over the wall and greets the king like an old friend. The courtiers are outraged. "He may be able to fly," they say, "but he is still only a barber." King Udaya says, "No, no. Gangamala is a holy man," and he asks the enlightened barber to stay and teach them. Gangamala says to everyone, "Meditate diligently and gain freedom for yourselves," and then he flies back to the mountains. King Udaya tells the courtiers that he gained his kingship through a small effort in meditation in his previous life, so they should never doubt the benefit that even small efforts bring.

Meditation is not easy because our minds are always either running after or running away from something. "I like this, I want this," or, "I don't like this, I don't want this." And however much "I want this," as soon as I get it I want something else, and then another something else and another something else. Then *because* these things are nice, it means that there are a lot of things that are *not* nice, and then you have to run away saying, "I don't want this, I don't want this."

As long as we have that way of reacting, our minds can never be at peace. So therefore, we need to learn that real joy is not in running after or running away from things, but in just being. Because if you just relax and allow your mind to be without having to get something or get rid of something, if you just rest, then immediately your mind will feel peaceful.

Peace comes with a certain kind of joy. Not like, "I've got something therefore I'm very happy," but a natural kind of joy. Just *being*. Like when we are in a forest or in the mountains or near the sea. And when there is joy and peace there is also, simultaneously, the experience of kindness. You just naturally feel benevolent towards everybody. And when you feel that, the mind becomes compassionate, peaceful, joyful and also very aware and kind of creative. And that state of mind is understood as the true nature of mind. Our minds are actually like that.

Right now, we have a disturbed state of mind, like water that's polluted and mixed up with all kinds of murky dirt and sand. And how do we clean that dirty water in a natural way? By just allowing it to be. In olden days they didn't have water purifiers, so they just used to put the water in an earthen pot and leave it for many hours. Then slowly, slowly, all the sand and mud sank to the bottom, because the true nature of water is clear. So that is the technique.

We are always very stressed because of running, running, running, so we need to be pacified and we need to slow down. But what can happen when we relax is that we might fall asleep or get into a dull state of mind, and that is not meditation. We need a balance: a certain focus and clarity, along with a little sharpness and understanding.

That is why I think it's a bit like driving a car. I am a very bad driver. I had very good teachers, but that didn't help much! Well, maybe they helped a little bit because I passed after my second test. But, maybe my tester was too kind. He didn't allow me to park, so I think I didn't really pass and that's why I haven't driven since I got my driving license. I'm very proud to have my license and I show it to everybody, but I never drive.

Teachers can help you to learn, but they cannot really teach you because you have to learn yourself. You have to have this awareness of what is happening around you plus a little bit of focus. And you have to also be a little bit relaxed. It's not something that your teacher tells you that you memorise, it is something that you learn by doing again and again and again.

Most practical trainings are like that. We need to do it again and again and again and then sometimes there is a feeling of, "Oh yes!" Just having a conceptual understanding doesn't work. It's not that you know anything more, you already know everything, but you know how to do it by doing it. Meditation is the same.

I think it is important to understand that meditation is not a very complicated thing. A great khenpo I had used to say, "Oh, there's nothing new to understand. It's very simple." So it's just like that. Just *being*.

When we talk about meditation or about taming the mind, we are more or less talking about shamatha meditation, which means calming down, pacifying, relaxing. You can tame your mind and become freer from negative emotions through shamatha meditation, but however deep and strong it can be, shamatha does not uproot ignorance and therefore it does not totally uproot negative emotions. Shamatha alone cannot take you out of the samsaric state of mind, so therefore you need vipashyana. That is the understanding from the Buddhist point of view.

Shamatha and vipashyana are not necessarily two totally different things, but for the sake of presentation, they are given differently and on slightly different levels.

Vipashyana meditation is about cultivating wisdom, which is the Sixth Paramita. *Vi* is one of the twenty-one prefixes in Sanskrit. *Vi* makes things "more", or "very much", or "completely". *Pashyana* means "seeing completely." So, vipashyana is about seeing the nature of all phenomena, the way things really are.

Sometimes, in shamatha, we say that an untamed mind is like a wild elephant. A person is running after this elephant with a rope and a hook, but the elephant is being ridden by a drunken monkey and the person, who is myself, cannot catch it. A huge and powerful elephant is not something you can easily control, especially if it's untamed. You cannot say, "Shoo, shoo," and it will go away. It is very stubborn. Sometimes it tramples everything in its path and then nothing can stop it, especially if it is ridden by a wild and drunken monkey. Monkeys are always jumping here and jumping there. They are not stable for any length of time.

«An untamed mind is like a wild elephant being ridden by a drunken monkey.»

Our mind is a little bit like that; very busy and active, a little bit out of control and quite stubborn. Mind is changing all the time, with lots of different thoughts and emotions, so if it wants to go a certain way, it is difficult to change course. If it is under the power of negative emotions it can do a lot of damage to others and to yourself also. Therefore, we need to bring some sense to this mind, some kind of taming or control. So, how do we do that?

From the Buddhist point of view, the only tools we have are awareness and mindfulness.

So, what is awareness and what is mindfulness? Traditionally speaking, awareness is usually translated as *shéshyin*. *Shé* means "know". *Shyin* means "continue." So, shéshyin means "continuously knowing." That is awareness. Mindfulness is the translation of the Tibetan word *tenpa*. It means remembering, being aware and also knowing what should happen. If I sit here and become aware of who is here, of the sun being there, of myself sitting here talking, just being aware of what is happening like that is awareness. Mindfulness is a little bit more than that. It is not only knowing what is happening, but remembering what to do, how to act at that time.

It is not just concentration. You can be very concentrated if you watch an interesting movie, but that is not meditation because you need to have an awareness of what is happening to your mind at that time.

Now these two are the tools for our meditation. Whatever practice we do, we have only these two tools. When we start to meditate, we need to know what is going on, so we need to be aware and we need to be mindful. In order to be mindful, we need to look at ourselves, to feel ourselves and feel what is going on. Therefore, meditation has to be looking in, aware of how I am experiencing now.

When I look at myself, many times I find that there are lots of thoughts and emotions going on, lots of inner dialogues, lots of wanting and lots of running after or running away from things. So what should I do if I want to tame all these fears and desires? First, I need to settle down a little bit.

Our mind and our body are interrelated, so if our mind becomes more flexible and tamed, it affects our body in a big way. If our body relaxes, then our mind relaxes, and if our mind is relaxed, then our body relaxes also. So therefore, first we relax all the different parts of our body. Sometimes we start from our head, relaxing our brain, our face, our eyes, our throats and shoulders and then move slowly down. Or you can start with your feet, and slowly relax all parts of our body, including our legs, our organs and so on. If we relax our mind, the body also gets relaxed. Sometimes we think it is easy, but, you know, it is very difficult for us because we are so habituated to being stressed. Therefore, we need to first learn how to relax. Actually, the main thing we do is relax, but not go to sleep. And not only not go to sleep, but not become dull.

The two things we always talk about are distraction and dullness. When our minds are busy thinking, doing, or reacting to something, it is called distraction. Our minds are busy because of what happened in the past, so we feel all kinds of emotions and worries about the future. It is said that if you are depressed, your mind is always in the past and if you are anxious, your mind is always in the future. If you are joyful and happy, that means your mind is in the present. Therefore, to work on this busyness of the mind, we try to not be in the past or thinking about the future and we try not to react to, or hold onto the present. Being aware and just relaxing is what we try to do. That is making our mind calm.

Sometimes people think, "Oh, I'm in good meditation," because there are no thoughts. We can sit quite nicely, in a kind of warm cocoon and yes, there are no thoughts and it is kind of relaxed, but it is not clear. That dullness is not meditation. We cannot progress, we are not training the mind, we are just getting into a comfortable kind of torpor. Like on a winter night, with a fire. Very nice, but that is not regarded as good meditation. Mind has to be clear. Meditation is training our minds to be undisturbed and relaxed, but not dull and sleepy. So, the meditation is relaxed as much as if we are sleeping, but also clear and vibrant, as much aware as if we are totally awake.

Many times we need some kind of focus. People often take something like a stone or a piece of wood as a focus, or they look at a flower or something on the wall in front of them. Something not so far and not so near. Something neutral, which doesn't generate too much emotion, otherwise you go into that story again. Buddhists sometimes use an image of a Buddha, or maybe a letter, or a colour like a white *OM*. White is bright, so therefore it is supposed to make you more aware, especially if you are dull.

People often use their own breathing as a focus. Breathing is dynamic; it is happening all the time. You cannot not breathe. You have to breathe, otherwise you will not survive. So, you are aware of the experience of breathing.

«The white letter OM.»

You feel the breathing in and breathing out. You know what is happening and you have a focus. As soon as your mind is distracted because of your habitual tendency, your mindfulness catches that and you can bring it back by just remembering the breathing. Or if you become dull and sleepy, as soon as you remember and become mindful you can come back. It is a kind of technique.

There are many different techniques to prevent distraction and dullness, but you have to do them in a relaxed, stress free, joyful way. I heard that Thich Nhat Hanh used to say that you feel that all the cells of your body are smiling. I found that very helpful because if you feel that all the cells of your body are smiling, then you have to feel quite comfortable and relaxed, because smiling is very relaxing.

There are many different instructions, and many different stages. Not remembering instructions is a problem, but it is also said that too much remembering instructions is also a problem, because you start judging, "Am

I doing that? Am I not doing that?" and then it becomes thinking. Sometimes it is better to have just one technique.

You know the story of the cat and the fox? The cat was sleeping in the doorway, and then the fox came by, and said, "Oh, you lazy cat."

And the Cat said, "Oh yes? What do you want?"

"I don't want anything. By the way, how many techniques do you know for escaping when a dog chases you?" said the Fox.

Cat said, "Just one."

"Ah, you are so stupid," he said. "I know one hundred and one techniques."

Then they heard a dog barking. The cat just jumped on top of a branch and said, "This is my technique. Now let's see how you use your one hundred and one techniques." And then many dogs came and chased the fox. He used all his techniques, but in the end the dogs caught him.

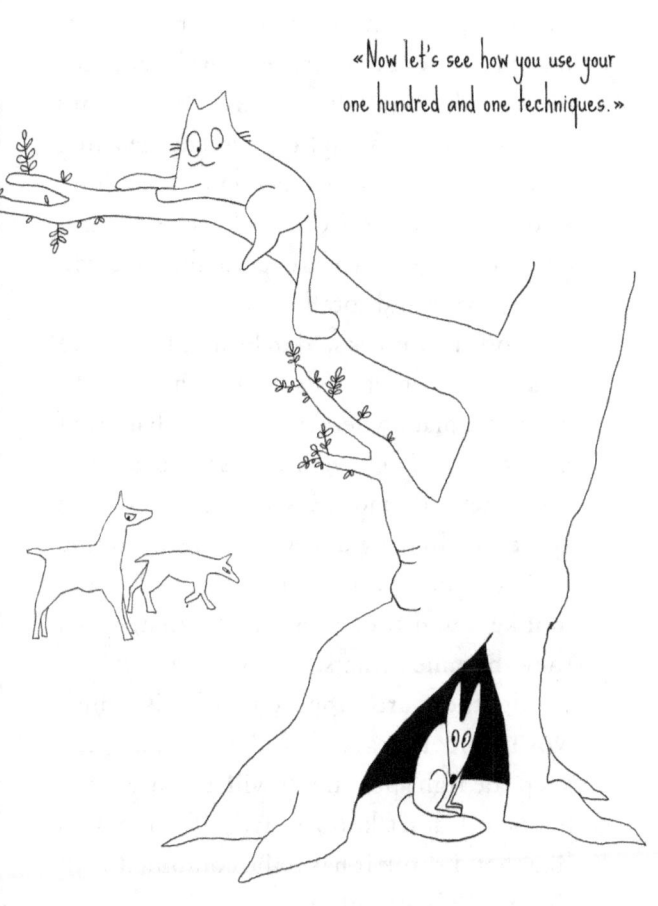

So, meditation has to not be about thinking, but more about being in this natural state of awareness. Relaxed, not distracted, but also aware. Sometimes people say it is eighty percent relaxing and twenty percent awareness. I don't know whether you can really find a kind of percentage in your experience, but you know, aware and totally relaxed.

Body posture is said to be helpful. There is a sutra, which tells how some monks went to a place where many arhats had been meditating. They went and sat down, and then they saw monkeys who had seen the arhats meditating and who were imitating their posture. So the monks looked at the monkeys and they also sat like that. Then they became arhats. These are not my words, these are supposed to be Buddha's words and he says that if you really can keep the right posture, it will automatically happen. I don't know exactly if it happens like that, I think it has to be combined with the state of your mind.

«They saw monkeys who had seen the arhats meditating and who were imitating their posture.»

Sometimes we talk about the seven point posture. The main thing is a straight back. Not just straight, but a straightened back. That is important because when we meditate we are supposed to sit that way for a long time. If your sitting posture is bad you cannot breathe properly and you can also create physical problems. But when you sit straight all the channels become straight. And when the channels are straight the mind becomes straight because your energies are in the right balance. Therefore, your breathing becomes better. This is the traditional Buddhist way of meditation. The right hand is inside the left and then the two thumbs are almost touching, just below the navel. This is mainly to make sure that your torso is balanced. They say that if your body leans this way or that way you may get certain good experiences at first, but then you get lots of problems. So therefore, your body has to be straight with shoulders back, sitting cross legged, with left leg inside the right leg. Buddhists call it *vajrasana* because Buddha sat in that way before he became enlightened. Maybe this is not so easy for everybody, but that is the tradition of vajrasana, or half vajrasana, the way I am sitting now. It is said that when you sit like this the weight of your body is not only on your tailbone but spread throughout your legs, and that makes the flow of your blood more balanced.

Once, I and my old uncle, who used to accompany me all the time, went to America. He had lots of pain in his legs, so doctors told us that he should wear special tight socks. When he wore these he could fly long distances and he didn't have pain. I was thinking that maybe sitting like this helps your blood to circulate better, because if you are sitting on a chair for a long time your legs get swollen very quickly. I don't know, but that is my own thinking. In the West, everybody sits on chairs, so to sit cross legged is difficult and sometimes very painful. I think if you have too much pain, you cannot meditate. You have to relax when you meditate, so if you have too much pain I don't think you can relax. Maybe you can train a little bit.

One important thing they say is that your tongue is touching your upper palate, so you don't have to swallow your saliva again and again. That really helps, because sometimes, when you don't know where to put your tongue, it actually makes you stressed. So, teeth a little bit open, lips a little bit open so that you can breathe from your mouth if need be, and that makes your face more relaxed.

Sometimes they say that if you can relax your eyes, you can relax your mind. So, eyes are not looking too far, not looking too near, not looking up, not looking too down. Now, this is also depending on what kind of meditation you are doing. If the meditation is to calm your mind, like shamatha meditation, usually you look a little bit down with eyes almost closed. If you are doing vipashyana meditation, or if you are dull and you want to make yourself more awake, then you look more straight. There are meditations where you look up, but usually, we look down.

Sometimes also people meditate with eyes closed, because if we are too distracted in the beginning, then it is easier if you close our eyes. But from the Tibetan Buddhist point of view, it is suggested that you don't close completely. The whole point is not to close down or have no thoughts, but learning to *be*. Aware, but relaxed. So that is why the eyes are a little bit down. And then also the neck is important. A little bit straight, maybe bent slightly forward so that it is balanced on your shoulders.

The image of the Buddha actually shows us the posture that we should try to maintain in meditation. This is the most common meditation posture, but as I said earlier, if you have a problem with sitting, then maybe you can sit on a chair. Maitreya, the future Buddha, is depicted sitting on a chair, so maybe I have to learn how to do that. I haven't learnt how to sit on a chair for the last sixty-three years. Once you get used to sitting like this, it is so comfortable that you cannot sit on a chair. So, that is the posture.

And then, you just go on doing it. Just relax, as I said. It is not so much about "I've done this, so now what?" but more about how calm I am, how much I am progressing within myself.

Sometimes, depending on how you progress, you are more clearly concentrating on the object of your meditation. Sometimes you are more relaxed. Sometimes you look at a very tiny thing. Sometimes you look at a bigger kind of picture. Sometimes you don't use an object of meditation. There are many different techniques and it is not totally necessary that you have to do every one of them, or in that particular order.

The main thing is clarity of the mind. Mind has to be clear, but not distracted. That is the whole point. And it's not that there should be no thoughts. That is asking too much. Thoughts will come and go, but you don't concentrate on the thoughts. That is where you have to train. If any thoughts are coming and going, you just focus a little more on what your mind is focused on and relax. Of course, you will hear sounds. If the bird sings you will hear it. If a truck goes by you will hear it. If somebody closes and opens the door you will hear it and if somebody walks up on the next floor, you will hear it, because you are not dead. That is okay. But you don't follow that. If somebody is opening the door and you are like, "Oh, why is he making so much noise? Every time I'm meditating this person is opening the door. He is disturbing me on purpose," then you are totally distracted because your mind is building a long story. So, you will see things, you will hear things, you will feel things. Different thoughts will come up, but you don't follow them. You just train to relax and not to look for some kind of experience. Not too much judgement also. Relax and aware. That is the whole point.

« Relax and aware, that is the whole point. »

Learning how to meditate is not in techniques. One has to learn from one's own experience. It is not that somebody can say something and you get it. Only by doing can you learn. There is no other way. And in doing that, you have to be a little bit mindful and aware. It is a relaxation, so not too *much* mindfulness and awareness. Now, we keep on doing this like drops of water falling on a stone, not saying, "Maybe today I'm going to get the result." Just doing. That is why we need to become friends with the meditation. You need to take this like your hobby, not like your job. You like to do it so you do it. No stress. Like your relaxation time, your time with your best friend. You look forward to it.

We want to tame our minds, which are completely wild and out of control. Slowly, slowly, you catch hold of your thoughts and emotions with your rope. Now, the elephant of your mind is roped and the monkey is a little bit tamed. Then the monkey is thrown off, and slowly, slowly the elephant is also tamed. This needs diligence, wisdom and mindfulness, and then your mind can slowly calm down. You know how to relax. And the more your distraction is tamed, the more you feel joyful, the more you learn to be yourself, your true nature. You feel peaceful, you feel joyful. Peaceful and joyful come together.

Many people think that being peaceful is quite boring, like there is nothing to do. But actually, if you really have peace it is very exciting because there is no pain of past things and there is no worry. So you are more joyful, and when you have become more joyful, then the mind becomes clear.

So these three things more or less come together. Peacefulness, joy and clarity. In Buddhism we call it *desal mitopa*. *De* means bliss. *Sal* means clarity. *Mitopa* is like non-thought, peacefulness. Peacefulness, joy and clarity become a very good basis for the vipashyana meditation. If you have this, then the only thing is to look and then you see, because the state of your mind is the way your mind is. But it is not good to talk too much about this because then you expect it.

"When is this peace coming? When is this joy coming?" Then it becomes like anxiously waiting for something, which is stressful and not meditation.

So that is the shamatha meditation. I don't want to say too much about the different stages and things like that, because I don't think that will help too much. We will talk later about vipashyana.

Questioner: There is a lot of sound distraction where I live, particularly from tree frogs. It's very repetitive like loud rain and I can't avoid it. Would it be appropriate to meditate on that?

Rinpoche: Yes, sound can be the object of meditation. I said anything is possible for the sense object of meditation. It can be a physical thing. It can be a visualized thing. It can be a sound. It can be anything, and it is also a tradition like mantras. Like reciting a letter like *OM*. I have never heard instructions to meditate on the frogs, but maybe you can, why not?

Questioner: Rinpoche, would there be a danger in getting stuck in shamatha? I have heard of people who meditate for thirty years and who have not really gained much insight. Is vipashyana an automatic thing that can happen when the mind is calm, allowing insight to arise? Or are we turning our intention to the motivation to have clearer seeing?

Rinpoche: I think from the Buddhist point of view, you have to do it. You have to learn it. It is not automatic because they say that you can be a million years in shamatha and not get anything. It is not necessarily that it happens, but it becomes easier if you have a good shamatha basis. With shamatha also, it is not that you meditate a little bit for thirty years and you get full shamatha. It actually depends from person to person and things like that. Cultivating a strong shamatha is not necessarily easy.

Questioner: Are you saying that no matter how much shamatha meditation you do, you'll never get there (if there is a "there" to get to), because you won't have uprooted the cause? How do you know when to start doing vipashyana meditation and how much of it to do? I know you are going to talk more about vipashyana, but can you say a little bit more about that relationship? Like should you do both every day or should you wait until you are stable?

Meditation

Rinpoche: There are different schools of thought. Some say that first you have to have a very sound shamatha basis and then go into vipashyana. Some say that is not necessary, you can do a little bit of vipashyana and shamatha together. Some even say that you should first approach with vipasyana and then bring shamatha in as a support. So, I think it depends from person to person. Actually, they should go together. Shamatha is mainly to calm and clear the mind, but it need not only be that. If you just see the true nature and you remain in that a little bit, that is also vipashyana. So shamatha and vipashyana are not two totally different things. It is not that when you do vipashyana, you give up shamatha. You do vipashyana meditation within shamatha, you can say.

It is said like this by Shantideva:

shi ne rab tu den pe lhag thong gi
nyon mong nam par jom pa she je ne...

Vipasyana, which has a very strong, clear basis in shamatha
Completely destroys all your kleshas.
Knowing that, first search for calm abiding,
Found by those who joyfully renounce the world.

So, the idea is that the two go together.

Questioner: Rinpoche, when you spoke about diligence, devotion and wisdom you said that wisdom is actually seeing the way things really are. Could you say a little bit more about those three terms and your explanations of them?

Rinpoche: Seeing things as they are is the wisdom. Devotion is more like certainty of the path. Because of the wisdom, you also get devotion, but this devotion is not just blind faith, it is understanding. So, if you understand that this is the way to practice and if you practice a little bit strongly, devotion is going to help you. The more clearly you understand, the more devotion you have. Therefore, the more devotion you have, the more diligence you have. The more diligence you have, the more wisdom you have. They are interrelated.

Questioner: I met several quite deeply committed Christian meditators and they all told me that you have to go through a very painful process of introspection in order to arrive at the light beyond, or whatever. I'm asking about introspection and looking into yourself and self examination.

Rinpoche: I don't think shamatha should be painful because we are just kind of relaxing and being aware. Sometimes, when we are studying – not meditating, but studying - we get a little bit frustrated because we cannot hold on to anything. We like to have something like, "Now I understand. Yes, this is it!" If all that is crashed, it can be very frustrating, but that is what Buddhist philosophy is basically like. Nagarjuna's philosophy of the Middle Way is to learn to not hold on to anything and not to cling to any concepts, so there is no position of "this is *my* philosophy." To understand that is difficult intellectually because in the end, you just have to give up. "Okay, it is nothing. I cannot hold on to anything." Whatever way you make a concept is not completely correct. So, when you deeply understand that, you have to arrive at meditation, not at philosophy. If it is philosophy, you say this is the way it is, but in meditation you don't have to say that, you just relax. The whole point of Buddhist philosophy is aiming towards a state of meditation where you do not grasp at anything and where you do not make a concept out of it. That is a little bit difficult for us because we are all used to being conceptual all the time.

Questioner: Rinpoche, can it be said that the mind that is full of thoughts and emotions is exactly the same as the mind that has clarity and peacefulness? Some people talk about a meditation mind almost as if that's a different mind.

Rinpoche: I don't think there is a different mind, but how you look at it, how you feel it, how you approach it, may be different. For instance, we feel that all these things are coming to us. This thought is coming to me, this experience is coming to me, and so I have to react to that. But when your mind becomes a little bit clear, maybe you understand that it is not coming to you, but from you. Now there is an arising of a sound in my mind, now there is an arising of a form, now there is an arising of an emotion. So if you can see that your mind is the space, then in that space lots of things can happen. There can be sounds, there can be clouds, there can be flowers, birds, storms and all kinds of different things, all coming within that space and all dissolving within that space, but it doesn't really disturb the sky. Space is too big to be disturbed by that.

6
THE PARAMITA OF
Wisdom

The final, or Sixth Paramita is the *Prajnaparamita*, the Paramita of Wisdom.

Jna means "knowledge," or "knowing," and *pra* is one of those prefixes which means "very much" or "complete." So *prajna* means "complete knowledge," or "complete understanding of the nature of everything."

From the Buddhist point of view, prajna, or wisdom, is very important because confusion is the main cause of our suffering. I have ignorance and confusion because of not knowing what I am and how things are. Samsara is created out of this delusion, and because of that, I have problems and sufferings and pain. Therefore, if we can develop wisdom, if we can know experientially the nature of ourselves and of all phenomena, then that is the end of samsara. That is why wisdom becomes extremely important. Sometimes it is even said that all the training in all the other Paramitas is in order to actually get the experience of wisdom. All the other Paramitas are leading to wisdom and wisdom can also help to perfect all other Paramitas. That is how it is understood.

Prajna can mean many different kinds of wisdom, even small wisdoms like knowing what is right and wrong. Having more clarity of mind, or a clearer sense of what is going on, is also wisdom. Knowledge and wisdom are slightly different. Knowledge can mean having information about different things and knowing different things, but wisdom is more about learning how to discriminate in a clear way.

There is a Jataka Story about the Bodhisattva long ago. It is said that he was a merchant leading a big group with their caravans and oxen chariots to a faraway place to sell their goods. But they had to travel through a big desert where there was a demon who would perform miracles and kill people.

There were actually two groups of merchants. They couldn't travel together, so they had a meeting to decide who would go first. The other group leader thought, "If we go first we'll reach the grass sooner so our cattle and oxen can eat first. Then I can arrive first and set my own price. If I get there late, demand will go down." So he said, "I will go first."

The Bodhisattva said, "You go ahead." He saw lots of reasons why it was better to go later. So the other merchant set off with his cattle and oxen and because they had to cross the desert, they were carrying lots of water.

When they were in the middle of the desert, a group of people appeared. Their clothes were drenched and they were carrying all kinds of things like fresh fruit and flowers. They said, "Why are you carrying so much when there is water just a little way ahead. Look, we are all wet."

"Look at all the fresh flowers we have."

"Why do you go on like this? If you throw this useless water away you can travel so much faster."

The merchant said, "That's true. Why should we carry so much? There must be water because they are all drenched and they come with such fresh flowers." So he threw out all the water and on they went. But there was no water further ahead and after two or three days they became very weak. Then the demons came and killed them all.

«Look at all the fresh flowers we have.»

And now, the Bodhisattva's group is coming to the same place and again these demons come drenched with water and carrying fresh flowers. "Oh why are you carrying all this water? It is not necessary, you know, there is water here."

All the people say, "Yes, it's true. We must throw away all this water and then it will be easier to go."

But the Bodhisattva says, "Do you see any clouds around here?"

They say no, there are no clouds.

"Do you see any forest around here?"

They say no, we don't see any forest.

"Do you see any grass, or green things growing around here as far as your eye can see?"

They say no, we can't see anything like that.

Then he says, "So how come these people are drenched with water and come with fresh blooms?"

They say, we don't know.

"There must be something wrong," he says. "I think they are something to do with this demon. We should not throw away any of our things."

So they don't throw any water away and they go ahead. Then, very quickly they find the remains of the others, all their chariots and everything.

So wisdom can be like that. But when we talk about prajna in the sense of the Sixth Paramita, it is more than the wisdom of knowing what is right and what is wrong; although that, of course, is included.

From the Buddhist point of view, everybody has the seed of wisdom and compassion, because that is our nature, our consciousness. That is why it is said that everybody has Buddha nature. That innate wisdom and compassion can be awakened and cultivated and limitlessly increased. And once our wisdom and compassion are awakened fully and increased limitlessly, then that is what we call a Buddha.

So Buddhahood is nothing more and nothing less than the full awakening of our own true natural qualities. Therefore, how to do that? Traditionally, we cultivate wisdom through listening, investigation and reflection, and meditation. These are called the three ways of developing wisdom.

«Listening is that we try to understand, or try to study the experiences of great, enlightened beings like the Buddhas.»

Listening is trying to understand, or trying to study the experiences of great enlightened beings like the buddhas. There is not only one Buddha; anybody who is enlightened is a Buddha. Listening here means complete listening, fully opening our mind and trying to really take in everything that these wise people are saying, without any judgment, without any argument, without any opinion.

Sometimes, when we start to listen to something, before that person is even able to finish his sentence we have already formulated our answer. We start to criticize or make a judgment even before we fully understand what that person is saying. Many times when I give talks, people come up and say, "Oh, I'm very happy, what you said is exactly as I think, thank you very much." It is just that we always want to confirm what we think we know. Sometimes, I feel that we all have a kind of box in our heads and whatever we hear or read from others we put in that box. If it fits then we are very happy, and if it doesn't fit, then we either find fault with it, or we reinterpret it.

"Oh what he meant was actually like this." So we cut the edges, we try to make little changes or else we just throw it away, "Well that's beyond me, I don't understand." It is no use if we listen like that, because we don't learn anything new. We are just confirming our own thoughts and our own way of seeing.

Once we have listened carefully, then we should examine it from every side. We should not accept it just because somebody said it, because then we don't understand and our wisdom doesn't grow. It is not possible to just believe and then have complete understanding. As soon as somebody has a doubt, we will also have a doubt and then we don't know how to answer that doubt. We do not understand, so we become full of doubts. Even if you have no doubts, you must investigate, because if we look from every side, we come to understand that if this is like this, it cannot be anything else but this way. So, reflection is very important. You can ask questions, raise doubts, look from different angles and you can debate. This is called reflection and investigation.

But even if you see very clearly that from whatever way you look, it is like that and there is no other way, it is still a conceptual understanding. It works on our way of thinking, but it doesn't work on our way of reacting. Because the examination does not become experiential, it does not totally transform us. For that, we need to meditate.

Now that meditation, that bringing of understanding to our experience, is vipashyana. We call it bringing your head to your heart, because it is not just an understanding, but an experience. Sometimes this is very hard, because that understanding really *becoming* our experience, and our reacting with that understanding, is the practice. That meditation is the meditation on the nature of phenomena. So therefore, if that knowledge becomes our experience, we have ultimate wisdom.

So, how to work on this? Usually, we talk about this in terms of impermanence, interdependence and emptiness.

Impermanence means everything changes.

If there is anything existing, anything that is compounded, anything that happens, anything that is grown, built, or created, it is changing. Nothing exists that does not change. That is the nature of phenomena. And how do things change? Things don't change only once a year, like on my birthday. Change doesn't happen once a month, once a day, or once an hour. We cannot actually say when the changes take place. Maybe the question should be, when do things *not* change?

Strictly speaking, we cannot say when change does *not* take place. It is moment by moment. We see light in a light bulb as being continuously there, but it is not like that. It is not continuous. It is off and on so quickly that we see it as one continuous thing. Everything is changing so quickly that there is no time when things are not changing. I think I am the same person I was when I was born, but I am changing all the time. Every seven years, all our cells are totally replaced, so I have not one cell remaining that I was born with. The mind is even more subject to change. What I thought just a moment ago is changing. Thoughts are changing, emotions are changing, moods are changing, everything is changing. Why is it changing so much? Because it is not one thing. I am not one thing. So many different kinds of things go towards making what I say I am.

Everything is either "dependently arising" or "dependently designated." Dependently arising means that nothing exists totally on its own. Everything exists because of many different parts, many different causes and many different elements. Each of these is also dependent on so many causes and conditions and elements, and each of them are also like that. So if we go down, down, down, it is really as if everything is made of nothing. That is why it is called "dependently arising." There is no one, truly existing thing that is the building block of anything. Because if there is one totally independent thing, then it cannot be affected by other things and it cannot affect other things. It cannot change.

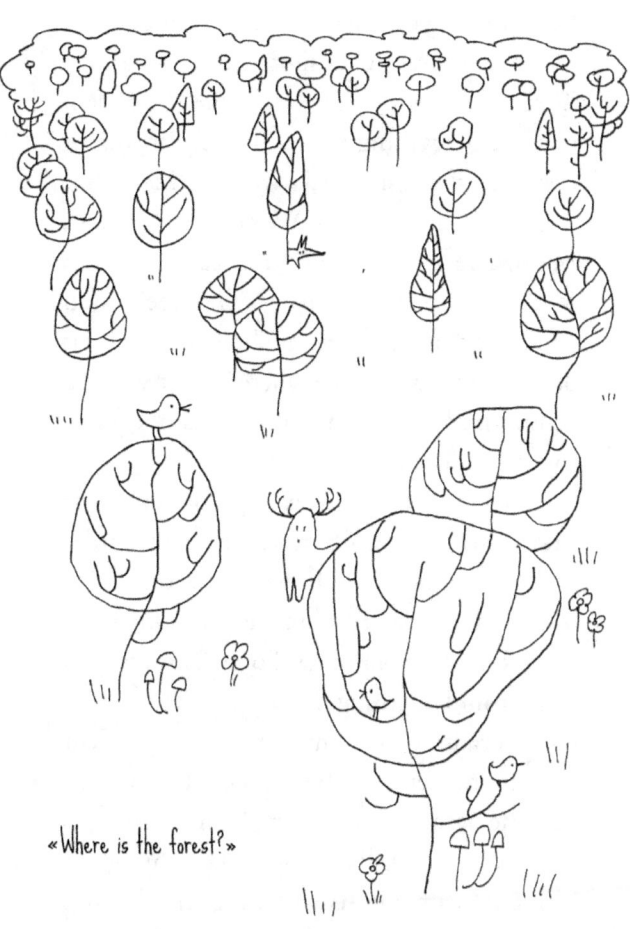

So if nothing can affect it and it cannot affect another thing, it cannot create anything. Therefore, everything is interdependent because everything is dependently arising or dependently designated. We say, this is like this, this is not like that. We say this is a forest. But where is the forest? You cannot find a forest in a forest, you can only find trees. But if you look at a tree, there are branches, there is bark, there is wood, but where is the tree? You cannot find a tree in a tree. You cannot find a forest in a forest.

I think that I am existing on my own. Maybe my skin is my border. This is my border and everything else is other. But actually, if I didn't have this air to breathe I wouldn't last more than three minutes. So in that way, you cannot find anything that exists totally on its own because everything is totally dependent and interdependent. Because of that, we say that the nature of everything is emptiness.

Everything is like magic, like a mirage. It is not a dream, but like a dream. In a dream I see everything. Things can happen. There is a long story- a journey you can go on. I can feel good, I can feel bad, I can feel pain, I can feel happy, I can feel joy. I can interact with people and everything. But when I wake up, where did they go? Where did they come from? There is nowhere to come from. There is nowhere to go. Was it there? Yes, it was there in my experience. But how was it there? From the Buddhist point of view it is called unborn nature. You cannot say it happened, but it was experience, it was there in unborn nature. You cannot find a building block of that experience in the dream. In many ways, everything is a little bit like that. Everything we can see, the world and the entire cosmos, is made interdependently and if you look deeply, it's as if it is built from nothing. It is appearance, but emptiness.

If that is how everything is, then why do we have to fear so much? Why do we have to be attached to things so much? Why do I have to react with so much pain and so many unnecessary problems? We are habitually caught up in samsara. I am afraid of bad experiences and I want good experiences. I feel that I am there, existing on my own. I feel that others are there, existing on their own.

So therefore, the more deeply I understand the way the whole of phenomena is, the more I do not need to react in the way that I usually do, running after or away from something with aversion and attachment and with lots of fear, desire and clinging. When that understanding becomes very clear to me, then I am liberated. I am free from samsaric bondage and free from ignorance. When I see the way I really am, I am interdependent, I am my consciousness.

What is my consciousness made of? If I try to find my consciousness, it cannot be found, yet there is consciousness. There is consciousness, but there is no "thing" there. So this consciousness is something that cannot be destroyed, because there is nothing there. That is why it can continue. So the meditation is to deeply understand that, and then to allow your mind to be in that experience.

«It is appearance, but emptiness.»

When our mind is calm and clear in a meditative state of shamatha, then in that clarity we remain in that understanding, which then becomes more and more clear and more and more experiential. That vipashyana meditation can then completely transform our way of experiencing and our way of seeing things. We know what is going on. We can react with clarity, wisdom and understanding. We know that it is not necessary to suffer. We can see people having problems, we know that we should help them and free them, but we also know that there is nothing truly happening.

It is like somebody sleeping next to you is having a nightmare. You know that this person is going through a very difficult, painful time, but you also know that there is nothing actually happening. At the same time, you want to wake this person up, because you don't want them to go through this experience, which you know is not actually happening. The more you have that wisdom, the more you have compassion.

That compassion is not focused on my suffering. The compassion is focused on others' misguided, misunderstood, nonexistent suffering. Therefore, that compassion does not need to be unpleasant, or bring suffering to myself. This is the understanding.

Wisdom is not so much an intellectual thing. The way things are is difficult to express and difficult to explain. It is not that whatever you say is right, or whatever you say is also wrong. We say that true wisdom is beyond concepts, but when you say "beyond concepts," it does not mean that it is beyond experience.

When Buddha attained enlightenment, he said:

Sab shi trö dral ö sal dü ma je
dü tsi ta büi chö shig dag gi nye

Sab means profound. *Shi* means peaceful. Profound, peaceful. *Trö dral* means free from all elaboration, or free from any extremes. Here, "extreme" means all the ways of grasping and all the ends of grasping. If you say it does exist, it is a grasping. If you say it does not exist, that is a grasping also. That is why it is called the middle way. *Sab shi trö dral ö sal.* *Ö sal* can be translated as clarity, luminosity. Extremely clear, it is extremely aware. And *dü ma je* means uncompounded. It is not something created. So:

"I found this Dharma which is profound, this experience which is profound, deep, peaceful, free from all extremes. Clear, clarity, luminous and uncompounded."

Buddha said, "I found something like amrita." This is a legendary substance in Indian mythology. It is said that when the universe was created, the ocean was churned with Mount Meru as the churning stick. The sun came out of it, the moon came out of it, poison came out of it and then at last, this amrita came. Usually, something that is good for your health is not very sweet. Or if it is very delicious, it is not very good for your health. But this is the opposite. Amrita is something very beautiful, very delicious and also completely liberating. If you drink it you become immortal. That is why it is so special.

Then Buddha said:

*Su la ten kyang go war mi gyur we
mi ma nag dab nyi du ne par ja.*

"If I explain or show it to somebody, they are not going to understand it. So it is better that I stay in the forest, in silence."

But after six weeks or so, he had requests,[2] and then he also wanted to know who could actually understand. So he went to Varanasi and sought out the five friends in practice that he had had before. And he talked to them and then they became Arhats.

Sometimes it is said that the difference between samsara and nirvana is misunderstanding; not seeing things clearly, not understanding clearly. If you understand, then it is wisdom, enlightenment. Not understanding is delusion or samsara, and then we have problems. Wisdom is not about getting something new that we do not have, it is just discovering what it is, what we are, how we are. Technically, it is very easy; experientially, it is a little bit more complicated.

Questioner: What would you suggest would be a good vipashyana meditation practice to do? How do you get to that deep understanding that you talk about? Just having an intellectual understanding is one thing, but will just doing a practice like vipashyana over and over again get to that deep understanding where actual things would be uprooted? Or is that something else?

Rinpoche: Sometimes we talk about analytical meditation and non-analytical meditation in vipashyana, especially from the Tibetan point of view. I must say that His Holiness the Dalai Lama doesn't like the term, "Tibetan Buddhism". He calls it the Nalanda system of Buddhism. It is thought that Tibetan Buddhism comes from Nalanda, where all the different types of Buddhism like Shravakayana, Mahayana and Vajrayana were taught and practiced as a whole. This analytical and non-analytical meditation came from there.

We try to see, try to look, try to analyse and then, when we come to a certain kind of understanding, or a certain kind of feeling, that is analytical meditation. Non-analytical meditation is when you come to a conclusion, or non-conclusion, or the non-findability of a conclusion, and then you let your mind relax in that. Non-analytical meditation comes after analytical meditation, when you come to an understanding that there is nothing to understand or nothing to hold onto. So you relax in that.

There is also what we call the Four Mindfulnesses: mindfulness of the body, mindfulness of feelings, mindfulness of the mind and mindfulness of phenomena. You mindfully look at what your body is, what it is made of. You are aware of your feelings, and of your mind, and then of all the phenomena. Not necessarily in a completely analytical way, but in a more experiential way. Human beings are basically very intellectual and so some analysis is good. Sometimes too much analysis is not very good, because then you become too conceptual. So, not too analytically, you feel and you look at those things experientially and understand.

Questioner: Is it that I could get to a stage where I see that I'm angry but that it didn't really come from anywhere, or that it started at some point and is going to end at some point, and so I can let it go? Or is there some other point to it?

Rinpoche: If you say there is nothing, it is just a concept. That is your mind making a designation or concept. And if you say there is everything, that is also a concept. If you say it is both, that is also a concept. Saying it is neither is also a concept.

That is why Buddha talked about "Eighteen Emptinesses." Because when he said, "Everything is emptiness," the monks said, "Oh, yes everything is emptiness."

Then Buddha said, "No, no, you are putting the symbol of emptiness on 'everything is emptiness.' That is just a concept. It is not like that, you know."

Then he said, "Emptiness of emptiness."

"Oh, we understand," they said. "Yes, yes, *emptiness of emptiness.*"

Buddha said, "That is another concept,

another kind of holding on to emptiness of emptiness. It doesn't work like that. It is great emptiness."

"Okay, it is *great emptiness* ..."

Our minds always want to grasp, but the way things are is not exactly like we usually think. You cannot say it is not there. Things are there, but how are they there? Kind of interdependently, dependently. My mind is also like that. Everything is like that. So therefore, when you learn to be, but not grasp, then more likely you will understand. All the teachings like Mahamudra, Dzogchen, Madhyamika are about that, so you slowly get into this practice step by step.

Questioner: What about love, is that dependently arising?

Rinpoche: What do you think? I think it is dependently arising, because it is dependent on many things. Why do most people fall in love under moonlight or candlelight? Because they don't see very well! So you need candlelight, and moonlight and you need to have an imagination. I'm joking.

Questioner: Could I ask you a little bit about prayer? Everything appears to be self-generated and dependent on our own efforts, but I suppose the concept of prayer refers to a reaching towards something outside ourselves. Maybe I've got that wrong. Is prayer in Buddhism also part of our own being? Could you explain, please?

Rinpoche: Generally, prayer is expressing a wish from the heart. In Buddhism, you pray to all the Buddhas, all the Bodhisattvas, all the enlightened beings, everybody who has wisdom, compassion and power to help. The prayer also has to be supported by a positive action. From a Buddhist point of view, if you make a positive action and then pray, it is more likely the prayer would work. If you do a very good positive action and make a very positive prayer, a positive thing might happen. But if you do a very good positive action and you pray for a very bad thing, a very bad thing may happen. If there is no support from a good deed, then the prayer will have no power. That is why you always do some positive actions before making a prayer, like a Seven Branch Practice, where you make prostrations, offerings, purifications, rejoicing, any kind of positive things. We pray to the buddhas and bodhisattvas of the past, because they have done lots of positive things. We invoke their power of virtue, their power of positive deeds, so that our prayer can become more effective.

Questioner: I wonder if the path to this understanding of wisdom is gradual, or does it have to be sudden at some point? Is there a gradual method that can be applied and does that method lead all the way?

Rinpoche: I think it is gradual. You practise and practise, and slowly your understanding becomes a little bit better and more clear. It may be possible that due to certain reasons, some people can experience or understand something directly, or quickly, or suddenly. Everyone does not necessarily develop in exactly the same way. Different people have slightly different ways.

Questioner: Can you say something about Empowerment?

Rinpoche: Initiation, or Empowerment is a kind of guided meditation. I would have received that Empowerment before. I prepare and I do some practice beforehand, I invoke the blessings of the lineage and then we go through the practice together as a guided meditation. It is like a blessing, going through the practice together. Once you receive the Empowerment, you are given permission to do the practice. That is why it is called Initiation.

From the Buddhist point of view, blessing is more about receiving than giving because there is no possibility that enlightened beings, or buddhas and bodhisattvas refuse to give blessing. It is not that buddhas are sitting there saying, if somebody prays to me then I give blessing. If they don't pray to me, I don't give blessing. Or, if you are a Buddhist I give blessing, but if you are not a Buddhist I don't give blessing. Enlightened beings try to give as much blessing as possible to everybody all the time, whoever and wherever they are. It is said that buddhas hate negative, evil doings, but they love evildoers. They love very negative evildoers even more. Not evildoing, but the evildoer. So therefore, there is always blessing, like the sun, which is always there.

Sometimes they give the example of a clear full moon night when one can go out with a bowl full of water and you can see a reflection of the moon in it. Ten people can go out and have ten reflections of the moon. A million people can go out and have a million reflections. A hundred million can have a hundred million reflections. After a hundred million the moon doesn't get tired, or become less clear. From the Buddhist point of view, blessing is said to be like that. If we have compassion, devotion, clarity of mind and an open heart, then we receive the blessing. You do not receive blessing from me, you are receiving it from yourself in a way. If we awaken our hearts, we have wisdom. That is the practice.

People ask, "Can I take part in an empowerment if I am not a Buddhist?" I think yes, why not? Anybody can take part. How much you take part depends on you. Some people ask if it is a blessing, or a real empowerment. That is also up to you. If you receive it like, "I want to get initiated into this practice," then you receive that. If you say " I don't want to practice it, I just want to receive it as a blessing," then you receive it as a blessing.

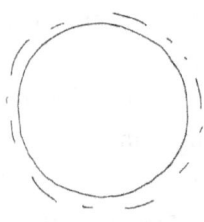

«After hundred million (reflections) the moon doesn't get tired, or less clear. Blessing is said to be like that.

Questioner: At the beginning of Vajrayana practice when we visualise the deity arising out of emptiness, have you got any suggestions about how to do that part of the visualisation? At the moment in my practice, the deity arises out of nothingness. I realise the importance of there being a difference between nothingness and interdependence, or emptiness. So have you any suggestions about how to do that stage of the visualisation?

Rinpoche: There are many different ways of doing the visualisation. There are elaborate ways of visualising, but then there is something like the Chenrezig practice, which is very unelaborate. We feel that the visualisation is there without going through too many stages. Basically, visualisation is working on our habitual tendency to see things as impure, with lots of problems, pain and difficulties. We are used to seeing like this; that is why we are here like this. That is our world. It is what we call our karma.

So, to transform this, you need first to allow your mind to experience something pure. That is why we visualise buddhas and bodhisattvas and all kinds of things like nice flowers and heavenly gardens. But we do it with a lot of compassion and a lot of wisdom, and a lot of healing power. You feel that everybody is healed, everybody is purified, everybody is transformed and that you are also. You *feel* your compassion, you *feel* your wisdom, you *feel* the positive experience of the buddhas and bodhisattvas and you feel your true nature also. If I can feel the presence of somebody who is completely kind and completely compassionate, who is very, very wise and who is radiating this kind of healing power, it can affect me. So I am actually practising to increase that kind of experience in me. I am transforming myself.

«Brahma requested the Buddha to turn the Wheel of Dharma.»

"Other than ending the maintenance of a sense of self, there is no Generosity.

Other than ending deception and cunning, there is no Right Conduct.

Other than being without fear of what is ultimately true, there is no Forbearance.

Other than being never apart from practice, there is no Diligence.

Other than resting in composure, there is no Meditative Stability.

Other than knowing how things are, there is no Wisdom."

Jetsun Milarepa

All my babbling,
In the name of Dharma
Has been set down faithfully
By my dear students of pure vision.

I pray that at least a fraction of the wisdom
Of those enlightened teachers
Who tirelessly trained me
Shines through this mass of incoherence.

May the sincere efforts of all those
Who have worked tirelessly
Result in spreading the true meaning of
Dharma
To all who are inspired to know.

May this help dispel the darkness of ignorance
In the minds of all living beings
And lead them to complete realisation
Free from all fear.

Ringu Tulku

Endnotes

1 On Buddhist observance days, lay practitioners often take eight precepts. These are also known as "one day precepts." In addition to the basic five precepts of (1) refraining from killing or harming living things. (2) refraining from stealing, or taking what is not given. (3) refraining from sexual misconduct. (4) refraining from lying and gossip and (5) refraining from taking intoxicating drugs and alcohol, practitioners would undertake to (6) abstain from eating after midday, (7) abstain from entertainment such as music and dancing and (8) refrain from personal adornment.

2 According to Buddhist tradition, the newly enlightened Buddha was concerned that humans were so overpowered by ignorance, greed and aversion that they would be unable to understand his teachings. Brahma, King of the Gods, was aware of Buddha's thinking. Fearing that the world would be lost if Buddha did not share his insights, he suddenly appeared in front of the Buddha and argued that those with "but a little dust in their eyes" would be able to understand, but that they would drift away for lack of the true teachings. He went down on one knee and requested the Buddha to turn the wheel of Dharma. Then, with limitless compassion and wisdom, the Buddha observed the suffering of beings in all the worlds, as well as their different capacities for understanding, and he agreed to teach. Brahma bowed low and circled the Buddha to the right, before returning to his god realm. Then the Buddha set out for the Deer Park near Varanasi, where he taught the Four Noble Truths to the five companions who had sought enlightenment with him in the past.

Acknowledgements

This book is largely based on teachings Rinpoche gave at Gaunts House in Dorset in July 2015. In addition, the chapter on the Paramita of Meditation draws slightly on teachings Rinpoche gave in April, 2016 at Kagyu Dzong in Paris. Also, the story that Rinpoche tells in this chapter on Meditation comes from the Gangamala Jataka.

I would like to offer heartfelt thanks to Ringu Tulku Rinpoche for his wonderful teachings and for his unwavering patience and support.

Thank you to Mary Heneghan for inviting me to transcribe and edit this book on the Six Paramitas, for her support throughout this process and for the Milarepa quote at the end.

Thanks to Karma Orgyen Namdreul for his illustrations, and to Minna Stenroos, who, as editing progressed, was more of an invaluable collaborator than a proofreader.

Many thanks to Donal Creedon for clarifying some points on the Paramita of Wisdom, and to Lama Karma Wangmo for her help with Tibetan terms used in the teachings.

Thanks to Tessa King and Jane Rasch, who organized the teachings at Gaunts House, and also to Kagyu Dzong, Paris.

Many thanks to Paul O'Connor for the design and layout of this Lazy Lama book and for putting it all together. Thank you also to Rachel Moffitt, who oversees the printing and distribution of all Bodhicharya publications.

In editing these teachings on the Six Paramitas, I have tried to retain the vivid sense of Rinpoche's voice and the way he communicates the dharma with such profound kindness and humour. Sincere apologies for any errors. They are all my own.

Karma Trinley Paldron

About the Author

Ringu Tulku Rinpoche is a Tibetan Buddhist Master of the Kagyu Order. He was trained in all schools of Tibetan Buddhism under many great masters including HH the 16th Gyalwang Karmapa and HH Dilgo Khyentse Rinpoche. He took his formal education at Namgyal Institute of Tibetology, Sikkim and Sampurnananda Sanskrit University, Varanasi, India. He served as Tibetan Textbook Writer and Professor of Tibetan Studies in Sikkim for 25 years.

Since 1990, he has been travelling and teaching Buddhism and meditation in Europe, America, Canada, Australia and Asia. He participates in various interfaith and 'Science and Buddhism' dialogues and is the author of several books on Buddhist topics. These include Path to Buddhahood, Daring Steps, The Ri-me Philosophy of Jamgon Kongtrul the Great, Confusion Arises as Wisdom, the Lazy Lama series and the Heart Wisdom series, as well as several children's books, available in Tibetan and European languages.

He founded the organisations:
    Bodhicharya - see www.bodhicharya.org
    and Rigul Trust - see www.rigultrust.org

Rigul Trust is a UK charity whose objectives are the relief of poverty and financial hardship, the advancement of education, the advancement of religion, the relief of sickness, the preservation of good health.

Our main project is helping with health and education in Rigul, Tibet, the homeland of Ringu Tulku Rinpoche where his monastery is. The Trust has previously raised funds for welfare projects outside of Rigul, however the primary focus of the Trust is to benefit the community of Rigul.

For further information and all the latest news please visit the website:

www.rigultrust.org

RIGUL TRUST

Cottamoor House, Haytor, Newton Abbot, Devon TQ13 9XT, UK
Patron: Ringu Tulku Rinpoche

UK Charity Registration No: 1124076

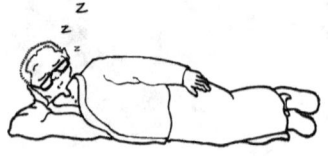

For an up to date list of books by Ringu Tulku,
please see the Books section at

www.bodhicharya.org

Our professional skills are given free of charge in order to produce these books, and Bodhicharya Publications is run by volunteers; so your purchase of this book goes entirely to fund further books and contribute to humanitarian and educational projects supported by Bodhicharya.

www.ingramcontent.com/pod-product-compliance
Lightning Source LLC
Chambersburg PA
CBHW070421010526
44118CB00014B/1848